PROBLEMS AND PERSPECTIVES IN HISTORY

EDITOR: H. F. KEARNEY, M.A., PH.D.

Britain and Germany
Between the Wars

PROBLEMS AND PERSPECTIVES IN HISTORY

EDITOR: H. F. KEARNEY, M.A., PH.D.

Titles in this series will include:

Britain and Germany
Between the Wars

Martin Gilbert, M.A.
FELLOW OF MERTON COLLEGE, OXFORD

LONGMANS

LONGMANS, GREEN AND CO LTD
*Associated companies, branches and representatives
throughout the world*

© Martin Gilbert 1964
First published 1964

*Printed in Great Britain by Richard Clay and Company, Ltd.,
Bungay, Suffolk*

Contents

MAPS

Acknowledgements

I am indebted to Mrs Fretwell for her skill in deciphering and typing my manuscript, to my wife for her useful comments and suggestions and to Richard Gombrich for the help he has given in scrutinising the proofs.

I would also like to thank all those who have given me permission to publish previously unpublished material, and Mrs Enid Chamberlain for lending me a copy of Neville Chamberlain's privately printed *Memoir* of his cousin Norman.

The Warden and Fellows of Merton College, Oxford elected me to a Junior Research Fellowship in 1962 which has enabled me to produce this book; I would like to thank them for providing a stimulating atmosphere in which to work.

My special thanks are due to Mrs Hendon Chubb of New Jersey, U.S.A., who in her ninetieth year has inspired me by her youthful enthusiasm.

Permission to redraw the maps has been given by Blackie & Son Ltd. for pages 81 and 119 from Mackintosh, *The Paths that Led to War* and Cassell & Co. Ltd. for page 49 from *Eden Memoirs*. The map on page 13 is reproduced, by permission, from *The Times*, 5 November 1962 and that on page 86 from *The Times*, 8 November 1962.

Foreword

'Study problems in preference to periods' was the excellent advice given by Lord Acton in his inaugural lecture at Cambridge. To accept it is one thing, to put it into practice is another. In fact, in both schools and universities the teaching of history, in depth, is often hindered by certain difficulties of a technical nature, chiefly to do with the availability of sources. In this respect, history tends to be badly off in comparison with literature or the sciences. The historical equivalent of set texts, readings, or experiments, in which the student is encouraged to use his own mind, are the so-called 'special periods'. If these are to be fruitful, the student must be encouraged to deal in his own way with the problems raised by historical documents and the historiography of the issues in question and he must be made aware of the wider perspectives of history. Thus, if the enclosure movement of the sixteenth century is studied, the student might examine the historiographical explanations stretching from More's *Utopia* and Cobbett to Beresford's *Lost Villages of England*. At the same time he might also be dealing with selected documents raising important problems. Finally he might be encouraged to realise the problems of peasantries at other periods of time, including Russia and China in the nineteenth and twentieth centuries. In this particular instance, thanks to Tawney and Power, *Tudor Economic Documents*, the history teacher is comparatively well off. For other special periods the situation is much more difficult. If, however, the study of history is to encourage the development of the critical faculties as well as the memory, this approach offers the best hope. The object of this series is to go some way towards meeting these difficulties.

The general plan of each volume in the series will be similar, with a threefold approach from aspects of historiography, documents, and editorial consideration of wider issues, though the structure and balance between the three aspects may vary.

A broad view is being taken of the limits of history. Political history will not be excluded, but a good deal of emphasis will be placed on economic, intellectual and social history.

H. KEARNEY

Introduction

This volume covers various aspects of Anglo-German relations from 1914 to 1939. It consists of short documents chosen from a wide range of sources: official treaties, parliamentary debates, newspapers, contemporary books, memoirs and private letters. The extracts have been selected in order to show the main development of British policy and opinion towards Germany and towards those other major issues which help to explain Anglo-German developments. The reader is invited to follow the controversies for himself, to see each problem in the terms and perspectives of its time, and to defer judgement, if he must judge at all, until he has seen the range of contemporary opinion and the method of contemporary argument. By studying the actual words spoken and written at the time of any controversy, the reader may be able to shuffle off the heavy cloak of hindsight which bedevils so many historical accounts of the inter-war years.

The Great War of 1914–1918 is often alluded to in studies of the inter-war years, but its impact is seldom brought out fully. The problems posed by the slaughter on the battlefields, by the growing bitterness in France, Britain and Germany and by the slowly emerging but tenacious optimism of the would-be peacemakers, are problems which constantly influenced the policies of the twenty years between the wars.

Dread of war and a firm desire to avoid such ghastliness again combined with a hope that war could be averted in future by some carefully constructed international machinery. The Treaty of Versailles did two things; it imposed terms of peace on Germany—terms considered by many Englishmen as harsh and vindictive—and, as part of the Treaty itself, set up the League of Nations, at whose meetings national differences were to be settled, not by anger and eventual war, but by conference and conciliation.

British politicians wanted to see Germany once more an equal partner in Europe; French politicians were afraid of a strong Germany and tried to restrict her recovery. President Wilson of the United States promised to guarantee France against agression, but in 1919 the American Senate rejected any American commitments in Europe. Russia, after the Communist Revolution of 1917, was too troubled with internal famine and political strife to play an active part in Europe. Britain, by this series of accidents, became the arbiter of Europe, able, if she chose, to try to keep the balance between France and Germany.

The reader can look at British relations with America, Russia, Italy and the League of Nations, and see to what extent British politicians sought in these nations or in the League a counterweight to German power. In 1925 Austen Chamberlain, the British Foreign Secretary, sought to bind France and Germany in a mutual non-aggression pact, with Britain as sponsor. But the Locarno agreement did not last. German ambitions grew with the growth of German power. Britain was not offended or alarmed by the re-emergence of Germany as a master-power; instead, she sought German friendships, and looked forward to good results from Anglo-German co-operation. In 1933 Hitler came to power in Germany. Although he treated Jews and Socialists with extreme violence, he said again and again that his foreign policy was one of friendship with Britain and peace in Europe. For those Englishmen who wanted Anglo-German co-operation Nazi domestic violence could be justified: it was the natural outcome of revolution. But once Germany was allowed to take her place as a Great Power in Europe, her sense of responsibility and respectability would lead to internal relaxation, prosperity and peace. England recognised Germany's right to demand a revision of the Versailles Treaty. It seemed absurd that a nation defeated in 1919 should be treated as a pariah after fourteen years. Germany claimed to stand as a bulwark against Bolshevism and sought to consolidate her influence in Eastern Europe. There was no reason why the Czechs, Poles or Rumanians should command great sympathy in England. A strong totalitarian Germany might be a more effective guarantee of security in Europe than unknown, inexperienced and distant small states: especially when the Poles had reverted to dictatorship, and the Rumanians to a dictatorial monarchy. The exposed geographic position of Czechoslovakia was not in itself sufficient reason for upholding the European *status quo* at Germany's expense.

The threat to Europe of Germany's growing military strength after 1935 was not always as obvious as it seems in retrospect. Britain might have been driven by it into the arms of France, or into a greater reliance on the League of Nations, but she was not. British policy, like British opinion, was divided, uncertain and prone to rapid change. The influence of what has come, rather loosely, to be known as 'public' opinion is always hard to estimate. Politicians have a choice: they can either bow to what they consider to be a public demand, or they can mould public sentiment to suit themselves. They might be unable to gain acceptance for certain extremist policies, but it is within their power to try to persuade, or to educate the public into acceptance of a previously unpopular or little-considered policy.

British rearmament after 1933 was neglected by the Government. The problem arises that if Conservative, Labour and Liberal politicians had explained the need to rearm, and had aroused enthusiasm for a more active and realistic defence policy, they might have obtained popular approval. As it was, Conservatives, despite a vast majority in the House of Commons, bowed to Socialist criticisms of rearmament, were frightened by the general semi-pacifist mood of the nation, and for five important years 1933-38, failed to dispel British apathy. The Foreign Office and the Generals advocated rearming as a necessary prelude to effective diplomacy—'negotiation from strength' —but the Government hesitated, themselves unconvinced of the need to rearm, and unwilling therefore to explain rearmament to the people.

Many British politicians were reluctant to believe that Hitler wanted war in the West; and they regarded war in the East as a potential benefit rather than a threat. They saw Communism as a greater evil than Nazism, and cited Stalin's vicious purges in proof. As for Hitler, he gave little evidence of personal madness, and in the section on Hitler I show how he could influence visitors to an uncritical belief in his harmlessness, and thus in his régime's harmlessness. He was often the best propagandist in his own cause. The Foreign Office, especially Sir Robert Vansittart at its head, warned against Hitler's ambition, but in vain. The Government never decided which way it would turn. Vacillation and indecision were frequently the dominant features of policy. Britain turned to the League and was disillusioned, turned to Italy and was scorned, looked at France and was looked back at with suspicious eyes, looked to Germany and was treated with flattery, respect and politeness. Britain's constant problem of how firm to be against aggression in distant lands, of how to decide whether to isolate Germany, or to draw closer to her, was constantly discussed, but only resolved in the last instance on 3 September 1939, with Britain's declaration of war.

Certain politicians expressed views on every problem and were active throughout the inter-war years—among them Lloyd George, who was Prime Minister for the last two years of the Great War and Winston Churchill, who was Prime Minister for all but the first nine months of the Second. The views of these two political giants are not always what one might expect; they show clearly the way in which opinions could swing and divide.

Most of those whose comments I have chosen were quite close to the problems they discuss, either as policy makers, justifying or explaining their decisions, or as critics of policy trying to make out as good a case as possible for their opposition. I have also sought examples of how each problem was seen in retrospect in the politician's reflections or the historian's analysis.

Where possible I have chosen forceful, brief extracts which reflect a substantial body of opinion, and which deal with an important aspect of each problem.

It is not the task of the historian to ridicule or to malign any opinion; his first aim is to discover how people thought and acted, and to seek reasons for their often seemingly foolish behaviour. In these extracts I have tried to show not only the wide range of British opinion towards Germany, but also how deeply divided and uncertain Englishmen were over the problems that confronted them.

The Great War

In the last British Government formed before the Second World War—Neville Chamberlain's Government of May 1937—seven out of twenty-two Cabinet Ministers held the Military Cross, won in the Great War. Almost every Cabinet Minister had served in the war in some capacity. The second youngest, Earl De la Warr, born in 1900, had served as a sailor.[1] Only one Cabinet Minister had been too young to serve—Malcolm MacDonald, son of the Socialist Prime Minister Ramsay MacDonald.

What was true of the Cabinet was true elsewhere—in the Foreign Office and the Civil Service, in the professional and business worlds, in journalism and in politics generally. The Great War was an experience that could not be forgotten. Its memory was an ever-present reminder of the terror of war.

In trying to understand the development of British policy towards Germany between the wars we must have a clear picture of the nature of the Great War, both as it appeared at the time and as it seemed in retrospect. The message of the war was two-fold: war was a ghastly experience that should be avoided at any cost, perhaps even at the cost of humiliation or surrender; but also, that if war came, there were in Britain reserves of patriotism and national unity to ensure that it would be fought with determination.

The dominant lesson of the Great War was the need to preserve peace, to attempt to build an enduring post-war settlement, and to ensure, either through the League of Nations or through national diplomacy, that future disputes would be settled by means other than by war.

DUFF COOPER wrote to his fiancée, Lady Diana Manners:

The attack itself was beautiful and thrilling—one of the most memorable moments of my life. The barrage came down at 4 a.m. A creeping barrage—we advanced behind it. We kept direction by means of a star, and a huge full moon shone on our right. I felt wild with

---

[1] De La Warr served in the merchant navy. As a conscientious objector, he opted for this particular form of alternate service.

excitement and glory and knew no fear. When we reached our objective, the enemy trench, I could hardly believe it; so quickly had the time passed it seemed like one moment. We found a lot of German dead there. The living surrendered. (*Old Men Forget*, p. 85.)

ROBERT GRAVES wrote:

The battalion cared as little about the successes or reverses of our Allies as about the origins of the war. It never allowed itself to have any political feelings about the Germans. A professional soldier's duty was simply to fight whomever the King ordered him to fight. With the King as colonel-in-chief of the regiment it became even simpler. The Christmas 1914 fraternization, in which the battalion was among the first to participate, had had the same professional simplicity: no emotional hiatus, this, but a commonplace of military tradition—an exchange of courtesies between officers of opposing armies. (*Goodbye to All That*, p. 121.)

Anti-French feeling among most ex-soldiers amounted almost to an obsession. Edmund, shaking with nerves, used to say at this time: 'No more wars for me at any price! Except against the French. If there's ever a war with them, I'll go like a shot.' Pro-German feeling had been increasing. With the war over and the armies beaten, we could give the German soldier credit for being the most efficient fighting-man in Europe. I often heard it said that only the blockade had beaten the Fritzes; that in Haig's last push they never really broke, and that their machine-gun sections held us up long enough to cover the withdrawal of the main forces. (*Goodbye to All That*, p. 259.)

LT. COL. GRAHAM HUTCHISON wrote:

It may be said that in this gruesome position in which were so many dead, dying and badly wounded, it was amusing to observe the German marksmen falling from the trees, with a heavy thump, to the ground. The moral effect of this touch of humour, which instantly struck all, was amazing. The wounded became cheery; the exhausted gained new life, and, as the 2nd Worcestershires, under Lieutenant-Colonel Pardoe, from reserve, swept forward to the attack and passed into the Wood, we forgot the heavy sacrifices which had already been made, and proceeded with rifles and machine guns in our turn to mow down the columns of the enemy. (*The Thirty-Third Division*, p. 17.)

NEVILE HENDERSON was in the British Embassy in Paris during the war.

The great thing about Paris was that one was constantly getting first-hand stories of what was happening at the front from soldiers on leave in Paris. The long casualty lists, the wet winters, the ghastly waste of human life in long-drawn-out battles with little progress to show at the end of them, was just a tragedy which left an enduring impression on one's mind. Did Providence give us an island in order to send millions of our young men to fight on the Continent? It always seemed to me that we had abandoned, to our great detriment, our traditional rôle of limited expeditionary forces such as Wellington's in Spain, based on naval and military co-operation. We had fought many wars on the Continent, but the number of actual British troops engaged had always been very small. We cannot dissociate ourselves from Europe, but it has always seemed to me a mistake to get too deeply involved in those far-off areas of it, where our sea and to-day our air power would be at a great disadvantage. (*Water Under the Bridges*, pp. 87–8.)

LLOYD GEORGE wrote in 1934:

There were few misgivings among the mass of the population in the victor countries when the familiar sound of maroons, which had hitherto been the signal for the passing of an air raid, now, on the morning of the 11th of November, announced the welcome news that the whole of the terror and ghastliness of a War which had spread over four continents had passed away. It had killed over 10,000,000 of the picked young men of the world in the flower of their strength, and crippled and mutilated many millions more. It had devastated entirely many renowned cities and fair provinces. It had shattered the intricate mechanism of international trade and left a welter of confusion and wreckage which would take a generation to clear and rebuild. It had poisoned the mind of mankind with suspicions, resentments, misunderstandings and fears which are still, and for many a year to come will continue to be, a constant menace to the healthy goodwill and neighbourliness of sentiment which are the only abiding guarantee of peace on earth. (*War Memoirs of David Lloyd George*, p. 1987.)

WINSTON CHURCHILL wrote in 1929:

The ordeal was over. The peril had been warded off. The slaughter and the sacrifices had not been in vain and were at an end; and the overstrained people in the hour of deliverance gave themselves up for a space to the sensations of triumph. Church and State united in solemn thanksgiving. The whole land made holiday. Triple avenues of captured cannon lined the Mall. Every street was thronged with jubilant men and women. All classes were mingled in universal rejoicing. Feasting, music and illuminations turned the shrouded nights of war into a blazing day. The vast crowds were convulsed with emotions beyond expression; and in Trafalgar Square the joy of the London revellers left enduring marks upon the granite plinth of Nelson's column.

Who shall grudge or mock these overpowering entrancements? Every Allied nation shared them. Every victorious capital or city in the five continents reproduced in its own fashion the scenes and sounds of London. These hours were brief, their memory fleeting; they passed as suddenly as they had begun. Too much blood had been spilt. Too much life-essence had been consumed. The gaps in every home were too wide and empty. The shock of an awakening and the sense of disillusion followed swiftly upon the poor rejoicings with which hundreds of millions saluted the achievement of their hearts' desire. There still remained the satisfactions of safety assured, of peace restored, of honour preserved, of the comforts of fruitful industry, of the homecoming of the soldiers; but these were in the background; and with them all there mingled the ache for those who would never come home. (*The World Crisis: The Aftermath*, p. 19.)

J. M. KEYNES pointed to one effect of the war:

In this autumn of 1919 . . . we are at the dead season of our fortunes. The reaction from the exertions, the fears, and the sufferings of the past five years is at its height. Our power of feeling or caring beyond the immediate questions of our own material well-being is temporarily eclipsed. The greatest events outside our own direct experience and the most dreadful anticipations cannot move us. . . .

We have been moved already beyond endurance, and need rest. Never in the lifetime of men now living has the universal element in the soul of man burnt so dimly. (*The Economic Consequences of the Peace*, p. 278.)

The impact of the war must have borne in upon Neville Chamberlain when he came, in 1923, to write a memoir of his cousin, Norman Chamberlain, who was killed in France in 1917. Much of the memoir consisted of letters written by NORMAN CHAMBERLAIN from France. In one of them he wrote:

Nothing but immeasurable improvements will ever justify all the damnable waste and unfairness of this war—I only hope those who are left will *never, never* forget at what sacrifice those improvements have been won. (20 May 1917.) (*Norman Chamberlain*, p. 140.)

NEVILLE CHAMBERLAIN wrote of how, on 27 November 1917:

Norman led his little band successfully to their objective, but here he and the company on his right came under heavy machine-gun fire. The ground was open, there was no cover, and orders were given to retire some fifty yards to a trench . . . whether the retiring orders never reached him or whether he was unable to get back, neither he nor his men were ever seen alive again. (*Norman Chamberlain*, p. 156.)

Neville Chamberlain lost a cousin; Rudyard Kipling lost his son. In 1923 he wrote the history of his son's regiment, the Irish Guards. In it RUDYARD KIPLING wrote pessimistically of the immediate post-war years:

'The Prisoner at the Bar,' as men then styled Germany, being entirely at home, was saving himself to continue the war underground when time, occasion and dissension among his conquerors should show him his chance. (*The Irish Guards*, p. 220.)

Ten years later RAMSAY MUIR, the historian, pointed to another consequence of the war:

[Britain] went into the war with a system of voluntary recruitment, which meant that the keenest and best of her sons went first, and were slaughtered in disproportionate numbers: perhaps it is as a consequence of this that in the post-war years there has been a perturbing deficiency of first-rate men, men eager to shoulder responsibilities and to face up to difficulties. . . .

A creeping apathy, a growing defeatism, a readiness to seek refuge from hard facts in a devotion to sports and other relaxations, seem to some observers to mark the temper of post-war Britain in a dangerous degree. (*Political Consequences of the Great War*, pp. 222, 223.)

The Treaty of Versailles

On 11 November 1918 fighting ceased on the Western Front. Britain and France had defeated Germany after four years of war. On 18 January 1919 the first Plenary Session of the Paris Peace Conference opened at Versailles.

LORD ESHER wrote on 23 January 1919:

The Conference is, by this time, a hotbed of intrigue—and a grouping of rival interests. How could it be anything else when all experience pointed that way? That was the overwhelming reason for not having a Conference at all. The moment you gathered together all these elements composed of men who have individual axes to grind in a city like Paris steeped in the old traditions, it followed that old methods would prevail and the procedure of Vienna and Berlin would be followed. This was intrigue, and the grouping of powers according to their pure material interests. The result will be a series of compromises and the sowing of the seed of fresh wars hereafter. A League of Nations will be a Holy Alliance under another name.

The German delegation was led by Count Brockdorff-Rantzau. His first speech at the Conference was made sitting down. Lloyd George was 'completely chilled by this one exhibition of inexcusable boorishness', but learnt later that 'the poor man was so nervous that he was physically incapable of standing up'. In his speech Brockdorff-Rantzau said: 'We are required to admit that we alone are war-guilty; such an admission on my lips would be a lie.' (*Journals and Letters*, vol. 4, p. 223.)

SIR HORACE RUMBOLD wrote to a diplomatic colleague from Berne on 17 February 1919:

There is every indication that the Germans have got their tails up again. The local specimens have reverted to their arrogant ways. Nothing could have been more insolent than the first portion of Brockdorff-Rantzau's speech. I hope the new armistice terms will be really stiff. (Unpublished letter, Rumbold Papers.)

H. A. L. FISHER wrote to Gilbert Murray on 1 April 1919:

I think that everyone here [in Whitehall] takes the common sense view that irredentist Germany would be of all Evil legacies to Europe, the worst, but we are not sole arbiters of the situation. Still I hope that our undoubted weight on international affairs may be sufficient to prevent an unprincipled peace. (Unpublished letter, Gilbert Murray Papers.)

J. M. KEYNES wrote to Austen Chamberlain from Paris on 26 May 1919:

We have presented a Draft treaty to the Germans which contains in it much that is unjust and much more that is inexpedient. Until the last moment no one could appreciate its full bearing. It is now right and necessary to discuss it with the Germans and to be ready to make substantial concessions. If this policy is not pursued, the consequences will be disastrous in the extreme.

If, therefore the decision is taken to discuss the treaty with the Germans with a view to substantial changes and if our policy is such that it looks as if I can be of real use, I am ready to stay another two or three weeks. But if the decision is otherwise, I fear that I must resign immediately. I cannot express how strongly I feel as to the gravity of what is in front of us, and I must have my hands quite free. The Prime Minister is leading us all into a morass of destruction. The settlement which he is proposing for Europe disrupts it economically and must depopulate it by millions of persons. The New States we are setting up cannot survive in such surroundings. Nor can the peace be kept or the League of Nations live. How can you expect me to assist at this tragic farce any longer, seeking to lay the foundation, as a Frenchman puts it, 'd'une guerre juste et durable'. (*John Maynard Keynes*, by Roy Harrod, p. 251.)

HAROLD NICOLSON wrote to his father from Paris on 8 June 1919:

I have every hope that Lloyd George, who is fighting like a Welsh terrier, will succeed in the face of everybody in introducing some modification in the terms imposed upon Germany. Now that we see them as a whole we realise that they are much too stiff. They are not stern merely but actually *punitive*, and they abound with what Smuts calls 'pin pricks' as well as dagger thrusts . . . the real crime is the reparation and indemnity chapter, which is immoral and senseless. There is not a single person among the younger people here who is not unhappy and disappointed at the terms. The only people who approve are the old fire-eaters. (*Peacemaking*, p. 359.)

H. A. L. FISHER wrote privately from Paris on 11 June 1919:

The moral atmosphere in Paris isn't encouraging. All the small States out for more territory and France is not unnaturally in fear of a revived and vengeful Germany. My own view is that passion still runs too high to get a really enduring settlement now, but that if a Treaty *tel quel* is signed there will be an appeasement and by degrees readjustments and modifications can be introduced which will give Europe a prospect of stability. As in 1814 and 1815 our own people furnish the chief element of cool temperance to the Councils of Europe. (Unpublished letter, Gilbert Murray Papers.)

The Treaty of Versailles was signed on 28 June 1919 by the Principal Allied and Associated Powers, and Germany.

The Principal Allied Powers were the United States, the British Empire, France, Italy, and Japan. The Associated Powers were Belgium, Bolivia, Brazil, China, Cuba, Ecuador, Greece, Guatemala, Haiti, the Hejaz, Honduras, Liberia, Nicaragua, Panama, Peru, Poland, Portugal, Rumania, the Serb–Croat–Slovene State (later called Yugoslavia), Siam, Czechoslovakia, and Uruguay.

Among the 440 Articles of the Treaty were:

RHINELAND

Article 42. Germany is forbidden to maintain or construct any fortifications either on the left bank of the Rhine or on the right bank to the west of a line drawn 50 kilometres to the East of the Rhine.

Article 43. In the area defined above the maintenance and the assembly of armed forces, either permanently or temporarily, and military manoeuvres of any kind, as well as the upkeep of all permanent works for mobilization, are in the same way forbidden.

Article 44. In case Germany violates in any manner whatever the provisions of Articles 42 and 43, she shall be regarded as committing a hostile act against the Powers signatory of the present Treaty and as calculated to disturb the peace of the world.

SAAR COAL MINES

Article 45. As compensation for the destruction of the coal mines in the north of France and as part payment towards the reparation due from Germany for the damage resulting from the war, Germany cedes to France in full and absolute possession, with exclusive rights of exploitation, unencumbered and free from all debts and charges of any kind, the coalmines situated in the Saar Basin as defined in Article 48.

AUSTRIAN INDEPENDENCE

Article 80. Germany acknowledges and will respect strictly the independence of Austria, within the frontiers which may be fixed in a Treaty between that State and the Principal Allied and Associated Powers; she agrees that this independence shall be inalienable, except with the consent of the Council of the League of Nations.

CZECHOSLOVAK FRONTIER

Article 82. The old frontier as it existed on August 3, 1914, between Austria–Hungary and the German Empire will constitute the frontier between Germany and the Czechoslovak State.

DANZIG

Article 100. Germany renounces in favour of the Principal Allied and Associated Powers all rights and titles over the territory comprised within the following limits. . . . [Danzig].

Article 102. The Principal Allied and Associated Powers undertake to establish the town of Danzig . . . as a Free City. It will be placed under the protection of the League of Nations.

Article 104. The Principal Allied and Associated Powers undertake to negotiate a Treaty. . . . To ensure to Poland without any restriction the free use and service of all waterways, docks, basins, wharves and other works within the territory of the Free City necessary for Polish imports and exports. . . .

Article 105. On the coming into force of the present Treaty German nationals ordinarily resident in the territory . . . will, *ipso facto*, lose their German nationality in order to become nationals of the Free City of Danzig.

Article 106. German nationals over the age of eighteen ordinarily resident in the territory . . . will have the right to opt for German nationality. . . . All persons who exercise the right of option must, during the ensuing twelve months, transfer their place of residence to Germany.

GERMAN COLONIES

Article 119. Germany renounces in favour of the Principal Allied and Associated Powers all her rights and titles over her oversea possessions.

Article 120. All movable and immovable property in such territories belonging to the German Empire or to any German State shall pass to the Government exercising authority over such territories.

GERMAN CONCESSIONS IN CHINA

Article 156. Germany renounces, in favour of Japan, all her rights, title, and privileges—particularly those concerning the territory of Kiaochow, railways, mines, and submarine cables—which she acquired in virtue of the Treaty concluded by her with China on March 6, 1898, and of all other arrangements relative to the Province of Shantung.

All German rights in the Tsingtao-Tsinanfu Railway including its branch lines, together with its subsidiary property of all kinds, stations, shops, fixed and rolling stock, mines, plant, and material for the exploitation of the mines, are and remain acquired by Japan, together with all rights and privileges attaching thereto.

The German State submarine cables from Tsingtao to Shanghai and from Tsingtao to Chefoo, with all the rights, privileges, and properties attaching thereto, are similarly acquired by Japan, free and clear of all charges and encumbrances.

Germany also renounced her pre-war Treaty rights and concessions in Morocco and Egypt (*Articles 141–154*), in Siam (*Article 135*) and in Liberia (*Article 138*).

The preamble to the Military, Naval and Air clauses of the Treaty reads:

In order to render possible the initiation of a general limitation of the armaments of all nations, Germany undertakes strictly to observe the military, naval and air clauses which follow.

These clauses included:

WAR MATERIALS

Article 170. Importation into Germany of arms, munitions, and war material of every kind shall be strictly prohibited.

The same applies to the manufacture for, and export to, foreign countries of arms, munitions, and war material of every kind.

MILITARY ORGANISATIONS

Article 177. Educational establishments, the universities, societies of discharged soldiers, shooting or touring clubs and, generally speaking, associations of every description, whatever be the age of their members, must not occupy themselves with any military matters.

In particular they will be forbidden to instruct or exercise their members, or to allow them to be instructed or exercised, in the profession or use of arms.

These societies, associations, educational establishments, and universities must have no connection with the Ministries of War or any other military authority.

SUBMARINES

Article 191. The construction or acquisition of any submarine, even for commercial purposes, shall be forbidden in Germany.

AEROPLANES

Article 198. The armed forces of Germany must not include any military or naval air forces.

REPARATIONS

Article 232. . . . The Allied and Associated Governments . . . require and Germany undertakes, that she will make compensation for all damage done to the civilian population of the Allied and Associated Powers and to their property. . . .

Article 233. The amount of the above damage for which compensation is to be made by Germany shall be determined by an Inter-Allied Commission, to be called the *Reparation Commission.* . . . The Commission shall consider the claims and give to the German Government a just opportunity to be heard.[1]

Article 236. Germany further agrees to the direct application of her economic resources to reparation. . . .

FISHING AND COASTAL TRADE

Article 271. As regards sea fishing, maritime coasting trade, and maritime towage, vessels of the Allied and Associated Powers shall enjoy, in German territorial waters, the treatment accorded to vessels of the most favoured nation.

Article 272. Germany agrees that, notwithstanding any stipulation to the contrary contained in the Conventions relating to the North Sea fisheries and liquor traffic, all rights of inspection and police shall, in the case of fishing boats of the Allied Powers, be exercised solely by ships belonging to those Powers.

GERMAN RESPONSIBILITY—'WAR GUILT'

Article 231. The Allied and Associated Governments affirm and Germany accepts the responsibility of Germany and her allies for causing all the loss and damage to which the Allied and Associated Governments

---

[1] Annex II (10) of the Reparation clauses stipulated that Germany should not take 'any part whatever in the decisions of the Commission'.

and their nationals have been subjected as a consequence of the war imposed upon them by the aggression of Germany and her allies.

GERMAN GUARANTEES

Article 428. As a guarantee for the execution of the present Treaty by Germany, the German territory situated to the west of the Rhine, together with the bridgeheads, will be occupied by Allied and Associated troops for a period of fifteen years from the coming into force of the present Treaty.

Article 429. If at that date the guarantees against unprovoked aggression by Germany are not considered sufficient by the Allied and Associated Governments, the evacuation of the occupying troops may be delayed to the extent regarded as necessary for the purpose of obtaining the required guarantees.

Article 431. If before the expiration of the period of fifteen years Germany complies with all the undertakings resulting from the present Treaty, the occupying forces will be withdrawn immediately.

On 28 June 1919, the Treaty of Peace was signed at Versailles. The German National Assembly at Weimar had authorised unconditional signature on 23 June 1919. AUSTEN CHAMBERLAIN wrote to his sister on 29 June 1919:

So Peace is signed at last . . .

Will the world have rest? . . .

Even the old Germany would not, I think, rashly challenge a new war in the West, but the chaos on their Eastern frontier, and their hatred and contempt for the Poles, must be a dangerous temptation . . .

But if Germany remains or becomes really democratic, they cannot repeat the folly of Frederick the Great and Bismarck and his later followers. No democracy can or will make aggressive war its year-long study and business, though it may easily enough flare up in sudden passion. But think of Germany with its 60 or 70 millions of people and France with its dwindling 40! I shudder! (*The Life and Letters of Austen Chamberlain*, by Sir Charles Petrie, p. 144.)

Sympathy for Germany was soon aroused by the news that German children were on the verge of starvation. HORATIO BOTTOMLEY told the House of Commons on 21 July 1919:

I am sorry to hear there are children starving, but I had rather they starved in Germany than in Belgium and in France. We have to look war in the face as a grim reality, and I believe with Sadi, the Persian

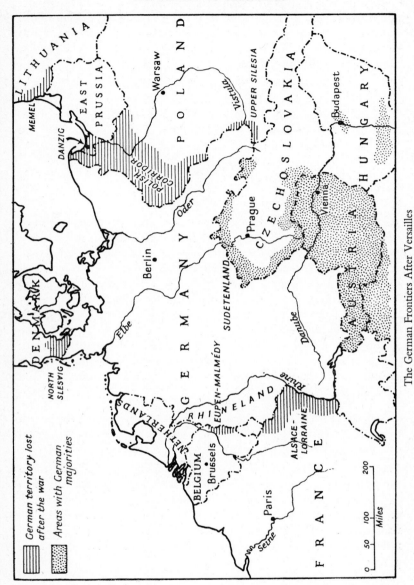

The German Frontiers After Versailles

13

philosopher, who said 'Showing mercy to the wicked is doing injury to the good; pardoning the oppressor is injuring the oppressed.' I was very struck with a line from Kipling the other day, which, I think, sums up this aspect of the case:

> 'These were our Children who died for our Lands.
>   They were dear in our sight.
> We have only the Memory left of their Home,
>   Treasured Sayings and Laughter.
> The Price of our Loss shall be paid to our Hands,
>   Not another's hereafter.
>   That is our Right.'

LLOYD GEORGE spoke in the same Debate:

We have restored where restoration was just, we have organised reparations where damage and injury have been inflicted, and we have established guarantees and securities in so far as human foresight could do so, against the repetition of those crimes and horrors from which the world is just emerging. We have disarmed; we have punished. We have demonstrated, I think, to the world for ages that you cannot trample on national rights and liberties, that you cannot break solemn covenants with impunity.

This is the task which we set ourselves, and I claim that this Treaty will be a lighthouse in the deep, warning nations and the rulers of nations against the perils against which the German Empire shattered itself. (*Hansard.*)

Of all the aspects of the Versailles Treaty, it was the problem of Reparations that troubled the post-war years most severely. WINSTON CHURCHILL wrote in retrospect:

The economic clauses of the Treaty were malignant and silly to an extent that made them obviously futile. Germany was condemned to pay reparations on a fabulous scale. These dictates gave expression to the anger of the victors, and to the failure of their peoples to understand that no defeated nation or community can ever pay tribute on a scale which would meet the cost of modern war. (*The Gathering Storm,* p. 24.)

This was very much the contemporary view in England. J. M. KEYNES wrote in 1919:

. . . I believe that the campaign for securing out of Germany the general costs of the war was one of the most serious acts of political unwisdom for which our statesmen have ever been responsible. (*The Economic Consequences of the Peace*, p. 134.)

LLOYD GEORGE emphasised the ill-effects on Reparations of America's withdrawal from Europe:

. . . as a result of the refusal of the United States to ratify the Treaty of Versailles, the only completely disinterested party was withdrawn from the tribunal. As a result the most interested party [France] is in the chair, with a casting vote. . . .

No person whose sense of justice was not drenched in prejudice could pretend that in its mutilated form it was either impartial in its composition or judicial in its methods. . . .

It is not a question of compassionate treatment of the vanquished, but of giving them stern fair play. It is not a question of straining the quality of mercy, but whether we are called upon to strain the quality of justice. . . .

Interpretations of the Treaty have been influenced by a small but bustling metropolitan coterie who never in their hearts made peace with Germany. (*The Truth about Reparations and War Debts*, pp. 26–7.)

Keynes's hostility to Reparations found many supporters, but the amount Germany had to pay was soon reduced. In 1924 the Dawes Plan gave Germany a greater say in the scale of payments, and brought American influence back to Europe. The concept of the imposition of reparations gave way, in part, to their acceptance by Germany in a more equable manner. On 16 August 1924 RAMSAY MACDONALD said:

I should like to impress upon the German people, if I might, that . . . we have created a system of arbitration, of examination, of revision, which will enable both them and us to observe the working of the Dawes plan; to watch projects that may be doubtful in their effects and to come together in a sincere desire to rectify mistakes as soon as mistakes are discovered.

In other words, the time of national isolation is ended and that of exchange of views and reasonable dealing with experience has begun. (*The Times*, 18 August 1924.)

Britain took a leading part in the scaling down and whittling away of Reparations.

On 8 July 1932 agreement was reached at Lausanne, whereby Germany was virtually freed from her Reparation payments. The German liability was reduced from 25 thousand million dollars to 2 thousand million, with the strong suggestion that even this remaining sum would not have to be paid in full.

On 15 July 1932 SIR HORACE RUMBOLD wrote from Berlin:

The comments of the German press are governed by the impending Reichstag elections and the result of the Lausanne Conference, which can only be described as very favourable to Germany, are not really judged on their merits. . . .

It must also be borne in mind that it is a German characteristic never to admit that any arrangement is entirely satisfactory from the German point of view. (Unpublished letter, Rumbold Papers.)

The virtual solution of Reparations did not end German hostility to the Versailles Treaty. Much of Hitler's election propaganda in 1932 was directed against it. In 1933 Adolf Hitler came to power, and demanded widespread revision of the Treaty. J. L. GARVIN, Editor of *The Observer*, wrote in 1933:

. . . the Germans, definitely superior in personal industry and in so many aptitudes for combination, seem as definitely inferior in political wisdom. There is no sign of psychological intelligence with regard to any other nation whatever. At this distance, it looks like one of the most extraordinary debauches of self-engrossed delusion that history has ever seen.

Alas, alas! The mistake, as personally I have never ceased to think, was not to have crossed the Rhine in full massiveness in 1919; not to have dictated at Berlin itself a more impressive and competent peace. They would have understood then what indisputable defeat means. They don't now. The psychological infatuation of their hereditary militarism was not thoroughly broken. (Unpublished letter to Sir Horace Rumbold, Rumbold Papers.)

British hostility to Versailles was often as violent as German hostility.

On 28 November 1934 EARL WINTERTON told the House of Commons:

Until Europe recognises and the Right Hon. Gentleman [Lloyd George] recognises that what is standing between Europe and peace are the conditions which were laid down in 1919, all the eloquence of the Right Hon. Gentleman will be nothing more than sound or fury.

Lord Winterton gave the House of Commons three examples of how Germans had described to him the Versailles Treaty—'that back-breaking burden'; 'that brutal instrument of torture'; and 'that cruel vice and grip'.

LORD LOTHIAN wrote to the *Manchester Guardian* on 9 May 1935:

National Socialism in its brutal aspects, both at home and abroad, is in considerable measure due to the fact that her neighbours were not able to make reasonable revisions in the treaties as war passions died down.

SIR NEVILE HENDERSON, British Ambassador in Berlin, wrote to Lord Lothian on 25 May 1937:

To my mind the British Empire is something infinitely too valuable to be risked for principles, which are not yet based on real justice. Amend first the injustices (and there are still some) in the Versailles Treaty and then, but then only, can we take a firm stand on the ideals of humanity and civilisation and of a true L/N. (Unpublished letter, Lothian Papers.)

Even Hitler's own behaviour was explained by reference to Versailles.

Commenting on the Munich Agreement, E. H. CARR wrote:

Herr Hitler himself seemed morbidly eager to emphasise the element of force and to minimise that of peaceful negotiation—a trait psychologically understandable as a product of the methods employed by the Allies at Versailles.[1] (*The Twenty Years Crisis 1919–1939*, p. 282.) The deep sense of guilt in Britain, which made people argue that Nazism was a product of Versailles, persisted through 1938 and 1939.

DUFF COOPER wrote to *The Times* on 21 March 1939:

Some of us are getting rather tired of the sanctimonious attitude which seeks to take upon our own shoulders the blame for every crime committed in Europe. If Germany had been left stronger in 1919 she would sooner have been in a position to do what she is doing today.

Duff Cooper's anger could not destroy anti-Versailles feeling. On 3 April 1939 IAN HANNAH told the House of Commons:

. . . I do believe that if we voluntarily expunged from the Treaty those war-guilt clauses it would be enormously appreciated in Germany and might help, to some extent at any rate, to improve relations between the two countries. (*Hansard.*)

---

[1] Winston Churchill referred to Hitler as 'this monstrous product of former wrongs and shame' in his famous broadcast of 11 September 1940—'Every Man to his Post' (*Into Battle*, p. 272).

America

From 1919 to 1938 America turned away from Europe. She had assisted in—perhaps she had determined—the Allied victory in 1918. The arrival of her troops in Europe, and their rapid success, suggested that America would henceforward play a leading part in European affairs. The Treaty of Versailles was permeated with American suggestions and American sentiment; the ideological content of the Treaty (for example, self-determination) was largely a result of the influence of President Wilson. But if Wilson had fostered the Treaty, his fellow-countrymen rejected it, and from the first rejection of the Treaty by the Senate on 19 November 1919, America drew farther and farther away from Europe.

HAROLD NICOLSON wrote in retrospect:

The whole Treaty had been constructed on the assumption that the United States would be not merely a contracting but an actively executant party. France had been persuaded to abandon her claim to a buffer state between herself and Germany in return for a guarantee of armed support from the United States. The whole Reparation settlement was dependent for its execution on the presence on the Reparation Commission of a representative of the main creditor of Europe. The whole Treaty had been deliberately, and ingenuously, framed by Mr Wilson himself to render American co-operation essential. (*Peace-making*, p. 207.)

President Wilson, however, did not have the mandate that a European might expect of an American President. He had been elected in 1916 as a result of a split in the Republican Party, and his views were not those of all his Democratic supporters. It was not surprising, therefore, to Americans, when the Republican, Warren G. Harding, became President in 1920.

On 3 June 1921 the first restrictive Immigration Act came into force in America. It succeeded, more than any international treaty could, in cutting America off from Europe. On 28 May 1924 a second, and more comprehensive, Immigration Act was signed by President Coolidge. Between 1907 and 1914 over a million immigrants had entered the United States each year. The Act of 1921 limited the annual quota to 357,803; the Act of 1924 further reduced the total to 164,667. This meant, for example, that the annual Italian influx—283,738 for 1914—was reduced to 3,845. In this way America appeared to have barricaded herself against contact with Europe. This move inevitably had international repercussions. America had retreated into her shell.

J. M. KEYNES blamed Europe as much as America for the breach. He wrote in 1919:

Europe, if she is to survive her troubles, will need so much magnanimity from America, that she must herself practise it. It is useless for the Allies, hot from stripping Germany and one another, to turn for help to the United States to put the States of Europe, including Germany, on to their feet again. (*The Economic Consequences of the Peace*, p. 135.)

America remained isolationist throughout the inter-war years. But in 1938 President Roosevelt did offer, on his personal initiative, to intervene in Europe on behalf of the Democratic States. Anthony Eden, Britain's Foreign Minister in 1938, wished to make use of Roosevelt's offer.

ANTHONY EDEN wrote in his memoirs:

I told the Prime Minister that we had been working for a long time in the hope that the United States would take just such an initiative. Chamberlain said it was vague and would fail. I replied that the President was just as well able to assess that as we were. He knew his own public opinion and this was probably as far as he felt able to go at the present time. Even if the initiative did fail, we should have gained immeasurably from this first American intervention in Europe and another might follow. I said that I agreed with Roosevelt's appreciation of the European situation and that I did not feel optimistic about our discussions with the dictators, though we should have a better chance if Roosevelt were also dealing with them. My view was that we should work on parallel lines, doing our best to improve Anglo–American relations while preparing for discussion with Germany and Italy. . . .

. . . I said that the questions raised by Roosevelt's message were so important that I thought we should have the opinion of our colleagues about them and I asked that Ministers should meet for this purpose. Chamberlain agreed without enthusiasm and said that he would issue the necessary instructions. On this note, a profoundly unsatisfactory conversation closed.

We were now head on and this brought out in Chamberlain's character a streak of ruthlessness reminiscent of his father, Joseph Chamberlain. He was evidently determined to see the whole of American business only in the context of his impending talks with the dictators. In this sense, Roosevelt, our French allies and I were all in the same boat. We were all held to be obstructing these negotiations, in which Chamberlain had dogmatic faith. (*Facing the Dictators*, p. 554.)

But Neville Chamberlain was not to be deflected from his course, and was supported in his rejection of Roosevelt's initiative by his close friend Sir Horace Wilson. Again ANTHONY EDEN records:

During the morning of January 20, Jim Thomas again saw Sir Horace Wilson, who dismissed the Roosevelt initiative as 'woolly rubbish' and made it perfectly plain that he was using all his powers to persuade the Prime Minister to pour cold water on the American effort, while going ahead with his own plans to appease the dictators. (*Facing the Dictators*, p. 562.)

On 18 January 1938 ANTHONY EDEN wrote in his diary:

I fear that fundamentally the difficulty is that Neville believes that he is a man with a mission to come to terms with the dictators. Indeed, one of his chief objections to Roosevelt's initiative was that with its strong reference to International Law it would greatly irritate the dictator powers. (Quoted in *Facing the Dictators*, p. 559.)

A month later, Eden resigned.

WINSTON CHURCHILL commented in 1948 on Chamberlain's refusal to take President Roosevelt into his confidence:

. . . no event could have been more likely to stave off, or even prevent, war than the arrival of the United States in the circle of European hates and fears. To Britain it was a matter almost of life and death. No one can measure in retrospect its effect upon the course of events in Austria and later at Munich. We must regard its rejection—for such it was— as the loss of the last frail chance to save the world from tyranny otherwise than by war. That Mr Chamberlain, with his limited outlook and inexperience of the European scene, should have possessed the self-sufficiency to wave away the proffered hand stretched out across the Atlantic leaves one, even at this date, breathless with amazement. The lack of all sense of proportion, and even of self-preservation, which this episode reveals in an upright, competent, well-meaning man, charged with the destinies of our country and all who depended upon it, is appalling. One cannot to-day even reconstruct the state of mind which would render such gestures possible. (*The Gathering Storm*, p. 199.)

NEVILLE CHAMBERLAIN wrote in his diary on 19 February 1938:

The U.S.A. has drawn closer to us, but the isolationists there are so strong and so vocal that she cannot be depended on for help if we should get into trouble. (*The Life of Neville Chamberlain*, by Keith Feiling, p. 322.)

On 19 March 1938 an anonymous letter was published in THE NEW STATESMAN:

There is no other people with whom Americans, in the mass, feel a familiar and reliable community of outlook and intention. England is the only country which could partner America into a genuine international system. Sever that bond of confidence, and American opinion and policy relapse into isolation. . . .

. . . let us choose expediency at the cost of international right and principles, and we shall render even the most friendly of American leaders impotent to bring America to our side in the international cause. (*The New Statesman*.)

But the Czech crisis, in which Britain accepted Germany's demands on Czechoslovakia, and even went so far as to put pressure on the Czechs to give in to them, further alienated America. The isolationists were confirmed in their view that to become entangled in Europe would be folly. When Germany invaded Poland on 1 September 1939 America stood aside; she watched France fall in 1940 without coming to her aid. She saw Britain stand alone against Hitler, but still refused to intervene militarily in Europe. Only when Hitler declared war on America in 1941 did America join the European war. All Britain's pleading had been in vain; it was left to Hitler to destroy the power of isolation. But Britain, by neglecting to gain America's confidence between the wars, had given the isolationist policy its justification.

C

League of Nations

The aims and machinery of the League of Nations were laid down at the beginning of the Versailles Treaty:

The High Contracting Parties
In order to promote international co-operation and to achieve international peace and security
by the acceptance of obligations not to resort to war,
by the prescription of open, just and honourable relations between nations,
by the firm establishment of the understandings of international law as the actual rule of conduct among Governments, and
by the maintenance of justice and a scrupulous respect for all treaty obligations in the dealings of organized people with one another,
Agree to this Covenant of the League of Nations.

Article 12. The Members of the League agree that if there should arise between them any dispute likely to lead to a rupture, they will submit the matter either to arbitration or to inquiry by the Council, and they agree in no case to resort to war until three months after the award by the arbitrators or the report by the Council.

In any case under this Article the award of the arbitrators shall be made within a reasonable time, and the report of the Council shall be made within six months after the submission of the dispute.

Article 13. The Members of the League agree that whenever any dispute shall arise between them which they recognize to be suitable for submission to arbitration and which cannot be satisfactorily settled by diplomacy, they will submit the whole subject-matter to arbitration.

Article 16. Should any Member of the League resort to war in disregard of its covenants under Articles 12, 13, or 15, it shall *ipso facto* be deemed to have committed an act of war against all other Members of the League, which hereby undertake immediately to subject it to the severance of all trade or financial relations, the prohibition of all intercourse between their nationals and the nationals of the covenant-breaking State, and the prevention of all financial, commercial, or personal intercourse between the nationals of the covenant-breaking

State and the nationals of any other State, whether a Member of the League or not.

It shall be the duty of the Council in such case to recommend to the several Governments concerned what effective military, naval, or air force the Members of the League shall severally contribute to the armed forces to be used to protect the covenants of the League.

The Members of the League agree, farther, that they will mutually support one another in the financial and economic measures which are taken under this Article, in order to minimize the loss and inconvenience resulting from the above measures, and that they will mutually support one another in resisting any special measures aimed at one of their number by the covenant-breaking State, and that they will take the necessary steps to afford passage through their territory to the forces of any of the Members of the League which are co-operating to protect the covenants of the League.

On 28 April 1919, the Paris Peace Conference accepted the Covenant of the League of Nations.

HAROLD NICOLSON wrote to his wife on 19 May 1919:

Look here, when you have *nothing* to do, will you please think sometimes about the League? You see, you have got to get a 'League Temperament'. Ready to help me when I become too national and anti-dago. If the League is to be of any value it must start from a new conception, and involve among its promoters and leaders a new habit of thought. Otherwise it will be no more than the continuation of the Conference—where each delegation subscribes its *own* point of view, and where unanimity can be secured only by a mutual surrender of the complete scheme. We, WE must lose all that, and think only of the League point of view, where Right is the ultimate sanction, and where compromise is a crime. So we must become anti-English where necessary, and, when necessary, pro-Italian. Thus when you find me becoming impatient of the Latins you must snub me. It is rather a wrench for me—as I like the sturdy, unenlightened, unintellectual, muzzy, British way of looking at things. I fear the 'Geneva temperament' will be rather Hampstead Garden Suburb—but the thing may be tremendous. . . . (*Peacemaking*, p. 344.)

LLOYD GEORGE told the House of Commons on 21 July 1919:

If one country, whilst being a party to the League of Nations, still goes on in distrust, not [trusting] in the League, not in its covenants, not in its public opinions, but increasing its armaments, how can *this* nation demonstrate its sincerity except at a risk which no statesman can possibly take? It depends upon the sincerity not merely of this land but of every country.

LLOYD GEORGE then answered criticisms of the Treaty:

I do not claim that the Treaty is perfect in all respects. Where it is not perfect, I look forward to the organisation of the League of Nations to remedy, to repair, and to redress. (*Hansard.*)

But with Germany not a member of the League, it was difficult to see who would want to initiate discussion with a view to altering the Treaty. For France, indeed, the League appeared as her best security that the Treaty would remain unaltered.

SIR SAMUEL HOARE said, during the same debate:

To me the League of Nations is not some visionary assembly of a new Jerusalem, but a practical body, sitting continuously, working upon concrete problems, and in direct touch not only with the Foreign Offices, but with public opinion in each country which is represented. . . .

To me the League of Nations, both in its conception and its constitution, is an Anglo-Saxon creation and an Anglo-Saxon ideal. Let not, then, the United States entrench itself in the Monroe Doctrine and retire to its own continent; let not also the British Empire content itself with the self-development of its own resources, but let us both together make the one organisation that is going to make the new world possible. (*Hansard.*)

LORD ROBERT CECIL told the House of Commons:

For the most part there is no attempt to rely on anything like a superstate; no attempt to rely upon force to carry out a decision of the Council or the Assembly of the League. That is almost impractical as things stand now. What we rely upon is public opinion . . . and if we are wrong about it, then the whole thing is wrong. (*Hansard.*)

Despite the enthusiasm of Lord Cecil and Sir Samuel Hoare, disillusionment soon set in, LORD ESHER wrote on 29 November 1919:

A war to end all war! Open diplomacy! No secret treaties! A League of Nations! Self-determination! What has happened to all these fine phrases that not one of them has been translated into the faintest semblance of actuality. . . .

But why gibe or complain? We have—that is to say the comfortable survivors—absorbed every German colony, we have annexed northern Africa, we have realised Rhodes's mighty dream, we have created or are able to create a subject Arab Empire, we may yet become the overlords of the Holy (!) City . . . The Archbishop and Bishops give glory to God; and Lord Robert Cecil is only as one crying in the wilderness. (*Journals and Letters*, vol. iv, pp. 247, 248.)

On 16 January 1920 LORD CURZON said in Paris:

The League of Nations . . . is not a mere expression in platonic language of the necessity for international friendship and a good understanding. It provides the machinery by which practical effect may be given to these principles. . . .

Should disputes unhappily arise, the disputants will find themselves in an assembly of impartial and unbiased Councillors, whose sole aim will be to remove misunderstandings. . . . (*League of Nations Official Journal*, February 1920, pp. 20–1.)

The First Assembly of the League opened at Geneva on 15 November 1920.

H. A. L. FISHER wrote to his wife on November 15:

I had my field day out yesterday having to introduce the armaments Report to the Assembly . . . the Report received no criticisms until we came to the last resolution which involved the Council to invite the Powers not to *increase* armaments (save in exceptional circumstances) for 2 years. This the French rejected—there was an interesting division, France, Poland, Rumania, Brazil, Chile, Uruguay voting for militarism, it was unfortunate that there should have been a division at all, but it couldn't be helped, and the French were very foolish not to let so harmless a resolution through. (Unpublished letter, *Fisher papers*.)

WINSTON CHURCHILL wrote in 1925:

Against the gathering but still distant tempest the League of Nations, deserted by the United States, scorned by Soviet Russia, flouted by Italy, distrusted equally by France and Germany, raises feebly but faithfully its standards of sanity and hope. Its structure, airy and unsubstantial, framed of shining but too often visionary idealism, is in its present form incapable of guarding the world from its dangers and of protecting mankind from itself. Yet it is through the League of Nations alone that the path to safety and salvation can be found. To sustain and aid the League of Nations is the duty of all. (*Thoughts and Adventures*, p. 252.)

On 9 November 1928 STANLEY BALDWIN addressed the Lord Mayor's Banquet in London:

Peace is to be made in effect by statesmen, and statesmen are fallible instruments, but nothing but good comes from those constant meetings of statesmen in the League of Nations. They learn there exactly what regard has to be paid to the peculiarities of individual personalities, and they can realize there what all people want to realize—that is to have the vision to apprehend the effect of environment and tradition on the men who come from countries other than their own. (*The Times*, 10 November 1928.)

LLOYD GEORGE told the House of Commons on 4 December 1929:

The League of Nations is in danger of being run by flapdoodlers . . . rhetoric is the petrol, but you must have the machine. But this is all petrol and no machine, and the result is that it goes up in the air and there is nothing but the perfume. When you pass through Geneva after the meetings it fills the air and chokes you, but nothing is ever done.

On 9 November 1929, RAMSAY MACDONALD addressed the Lord Mayor's Banquet in London:

The League of Nations grows in moral courage. Its frown will soon be more dreaded than a nation's arms, and when that happens you and I shall have security and peace. (*The Times*, 10 November 1929.)

On 10 March 1931 Germany and Austria signed the Vienna Protocol, in which they announced that they would negotiate a Treaty 'to assimilate the tariffs and economic policies' of their respective countries. On 16 May 1931 France challenged this attempt to create an Austro-German economic union. On 15 September 1931 the Permanent Court of International Justice, by eight votes to seven, declared the proposed Austro-German Treaty 'not compatible' with the Geneva Protocol. The Treaty was abandoned. League 'justice' had been done. Article 80 of the Versailles Treaty remained unviolated.

Six days later, on 21 September, the League was faced with a more distant and greater problem. China appealed to the League against Japanese aggression. The American Secretary of State promised 'to reinforce what the League does'—a virtual return of America to the League on this particular issue. On 24 October the League called upon

Japan to withdraw its troops. Japan refused, and on 10 December the League set up a Commission of Five 'to study on the spot'. More information was needed before specific action could be taken against Japan.

SIR AUSTEN CHAMBERLAIN told the House of Commons on 22 March 1932:

I am no believer in the development of the League of Nations by force. The less we hear of the sanctions of the League the stronger its moral authority will be, and unless its moral authority be strong, whatever the sanctions are they will not prevent war. . . . Patience, consideration, conciliation, time, those are the weapons of the League, and its sanction is the moral condemnation of the world. (*Hansard*.)

Though British opinion disliked Japan's aggressive mood, many refused to go from dislike to condemnation. WINSTON CHURCHILL spoke up, on 17 February 1933, for the unpopular, but not necessarily minority view:

Now I must say something to you which is very unfashionable. I am going to say one word of sympathy for Japan, not necessarily for her policy, but for her position and her national difficulties. I do not think the League of Nations would be well-advised to quarrel with Japan. The League has a great work to do in Europe. . . .

There is no more use affronting Japan than there would be in ordering the Swiss and Czechoslovak navies to the yellow sea. . . .

I hope we in England shall try to understand a little the position of Japan, an ancient State, with the highest sense of national honour and patriotism, and with a teeming population and a remarkable energy. On the one side they see the dark menace of Soviet Russia. On the other the chaos of China . . . (Quoted in, *Democracy and Foreign Policy*, by R. Bassett, p. 564.)

The League could not stop the war. It had responded quickly, but its response was to comment rather than to act. On 28 January 1932 the Japanese bombed Shanghai, where Britain and America had territorial concessions and trading rights. Finding their interests threatened directly, Britain and America acted swiftly, and independently of the League. SIR JOHN SIMON told the House of Commons on 2 February 1932:

His Majesty's Government regard these events with grave concern, both in the general interests of peace and owing to the proximity of the

International Settlement, with the consequent danger to the lives and properties of British nationals. We have lost no time in making pressing representations. (*Hansard*.)

Neither Britain alone nor the League could restrain Japan in Manchuria. On 1 March 1932 the Japanese announced the establishment of a new state—Manchukuo, conquered from the Chinese provinces of Manchuria and Mongolia. In Shanghai China and Japan reached agreement, with the assistance of the British, American, French and Italian Ministers. The Japanese Foreign Minister Viscount Saito praised, on 3 June 1932, 'the earnest labours of the British Minister to China . . . as well as our own attitude of fairness and rectitude'. On 4 September 1932 the League Inquiry Commission published its report. It severely criticised but refused to 'condemn' the Japanese establishment of the Manchukuo State. But Manchukuo was not returned to China until Japan was defeated in 1946.

The League of Nations turned from Japan to disarmament. But it failed to obtain agreement for even the smallest measure of an international reduction of arms. Thomas Jones, a close friend of Stanley Baldwin's, thought that personal as well as national considerations were responsible.

On 27 September 1932 THOMAS JONES wrote to a friend:

What you say about Simon is borne out on all sides. I am told 'he has reduced Geneva to immobility'. . . . Everybody distrusts everybody. The major powers have brought with them the 'Old Diplomacy'; their Foreign Offices and still more their Fighting Departments are hostile to the League and bent on making Disarmament a farce. The French want more guarantees of security especially from U.S.A; the Germans are in confusion. . . . Italy does not want to disarm except in the sense of being equally armed with France, and is busily arming the *minds* of the people; no-one is sure what Russia is doing; England all this year has been negative and this want of moral leadership has infected the rest. (*A Diary With Letters*, p. 63.)

In 1933 the League's discussions were complicated by the emergence of Nazi Government in Germany. By the end of the year Nazi opinions were being advocated at Geneva by the official German delegate, and by Dr Goebbels, the German Minister for Propaganda, who paid Geneva a special visit. The British delegate, WILLIAM ORMSBY-GORE spoke out against the new Nazi doctrines.

Wherever the Jews have been well and liberally treated, they have been the most loyal and helpful members of the nation.

In view of the attention which this question is attracting throughout the world, people in England are reading what Chancellor Hitler has written on the subject and are trying to understand the German point of view. What we read, quite frankly, makes us nervous. . . .

Look at the British Empire: people of every race, every colour, every creed! Why, even in our own little island of Great Britain we have a population of the most mixed stock. Ever since neolithic times there has been an infiltration into Britain of various races and strains from all over the world. Frankly, this Aryan doctrine . . . cannot apply to the British Empire. (*League of Nations Official Journal 1933*, Special Supplement No. 120, pp. 34–7.)

Ormsby-Gore was outspoken. The League was not a mere platform for platitudes. In a private letter ORMSBY-GORE revealed even more clearly how shocked he was by the new German attitude:

The significant feature of this Assembly is the arrogance and aggressiveness of the Germans—Goebbels' bodyguard of cut throats—display of swastikas and brusque brutality. They initiated the Jewish question and were the first to raise it in a most challenging manner—and they commended the doctrine of 'Volkstum' to the League of Nations!

I see that in their new control of their press by excluding all non-Aryans from the journalist profession they insist on requesting all journalists, among other things, to write nothing that would prejudice 'German military preparedness'.

My own deductions from many neighbours of Germany that I have spoken to is that whatever they may say in public to the contrary, they are preparing materially, psychologically and educationally for another war. France is much to be blamed for the past—but to disarm her now in face of this new challenge is to endanger not merely peace but the liberties and decencies of humanity.

It is remarkable how all the small nations especially—like Holland, Sweden, Switzerland, etc., are rallying against the new German menace to the fundamental bases of civilisation and the rights of man. The truth is that the German *princes* were more liberal, tolerant, and peace loving than the German people. Unless we all stand firm against the new menace of reaction, all we care for in Europe is doomed. (Unpublished letter to Gilbert Murray, Gilbert Murray Papers.)

The League's inability to act against Japan in 1932 posed two problems for Britain. Would not each nation have to act on its own, or with a few specially chosen allies, if it wished to act at all in similar circumstances. And might not the League condemn a nation—as it had condemned Japan—which Britain did not think ought to be condemned?

The test case arose when fighting broke out in the border of Abyssinia and Italian Somaliland—at Walwal—on 5 December 1934.

The Abyssinian Government appealed to the League for assistance against Italy on 14 December. The League postponed its decision indefinitely. Britain, meanwhile, acted independently of the League when Anthony Eden visited Mussolini in Rome in June 1935 and put forward compromise proposals which Mussolini, unfortunately for Britain, rejected.

SIR SAMUEL HOARE defended Eden's visit to Rome on 11 July 1935 in the House of Commons:

The Government feel that they took the only course that was open. . . . I say to those who profess their belief in the League of Nations that it is an obligation upon us when we see the system of the League of Nations threatened, to make constructive proposals, if we can find them, for avoiding what we believe would be a calamity. It is in that spirit that my Right Hon. friend went to Rome. (*Hansard*.)

ANTHONY EDEN recalled his visit in his Memoirs:

Mussolini seemed fixed in purpose and impervious to the evident dangers. We [Eric Drummond, William Strang and Eden] agreed that I should so report to my colleagues, who should now have to determine their course between upholding the League and losing an ally, or undermining the foundation of peace in Europe. The series of pacts and agreement which criss-crossed Europe were, almost all of them, related to the League. If it were once shown that these engagements were of no avail when a great power wanted to swallow a smaller one, confidence would be shattered and the temptation to make terms with the biggest bully in the neighbourhood would be irresistible. (*Facing the Dictators*, pp. 228–9.)

Some Englishmen wanted more powerful action on Britain's part. On 1 August 1935 SIR SAMUEL HOARE answered them in the Commons:

It is easy, and perhaps it is tempting, in a controversy of this kind to jump into the arena impetuously and rashly, to throw down your glove and to challenge anyone who disagrees with you to fight. Supposing, however, that your action destroyed for years the basis of international-cooperation, supposing the result of your action was to cripple and mutilate the League for a generation to come, your rashness, however courageous, would be foolish to the point of criminal folly. (*Hansard.*)

On 2 October 1935, Italy invaded Abyssinia. On 10 October ANTHONY EDEN addressed the League Assembly:

The League has two main tasks. First, to avert war by the just and peaceful settlement of all disputes. Secondly, if we fail in our first objective, to stop war . . . it is by the League's effectiveness in realizing this aim that the League will be judged. We cannot neglect our duties and responsibilities. Action must now be taken. . . . On behalf of His Majesty's Government in the United Kingdom I declare our willingness to take our full part in such action. . . . War is at this moment actually in progress. We must therefore persist in the action which our obligations under the Covenant command us to assume. (*League of Nations Official Journal*, Special Supplement No. 136, p. 106.)

On 22 October 1935 SIR SAMUEL HOARE told the House of Commons:

If the League does fail, the world at large, and Europe in particular, will be faced with a period of almost unrelieved danger and gloom.

But of oil sanctions (which Eden considered essential) HOARE was critical:

The pre-condition for the enforcement of such sanctions, namely collective agreement at Geneva, has never existed. . . . We are not prepared, and we do not intend, to act alone. . . . The League, let us remember, is a great instrument of peace. Let the critics remember this fact when they say that we ought to block up the Suez Canal and cut the Italian communications. (*Hansard.*)

WINSTON CHURCHILL was in favour of sanctions—'of striking a decisive blow', as he wrote in 1946, 'with the minimum of risk'. (*The Gathering Storm*, p. 138.)

He told the House of Commons on 23 October 1935:

We have moved on, and we are not going to move back. The League of Nations has passed from shadow into substance, from theory into practice, from rhetoric into reality. We see a structure always majestic, but hitherto shadowy, which is now being clothed with life and power, and endowed with coherent thought and concerted action. (*Hansard.*)

In December 1935 Eden urged the British Cabinet to accept oil sanctions which, he claimed, would force Italy to stop hostilities. The danger of Mussolini attacking England in retaliation was, he said, 'very remote'.

Eden's view seems confirmed by a conversation recalled by Paul Schmidt, Hitler's interpreter, in 1951. According to Schmidt, MUSSOLINI told Hitler in 1938:

If the League of Nations had followed Eden's advice . . . and had extended economic sanctions to oil, I would have had to withdraw from Abyssinia within a week. (Paul Schmidt, *Hitler's Interpreter*, Heinemann, 1951.)

On 7 December 1935 Sir Samuel Hoare met Pierre Laval, the French Foreign Minister, in Paris. They issued a statement saying that they had sought a solution to the Abyssinian war. Next day their proposed solution was published in the Press: Italy was to have parts of Abyssinia while Abyssinia was to receive a corridor to the sea—without, however, being allowed to build a railway on it. The public outcry at this plan— 'Selling Abyssinia to Italy' and 'Running behind the League's back'— led to Hoare's resignation. Eden became Foreign Secretary. The League agreed upon economic sanctions generally, but postponed any decision on the most important economic sanction—oil. On 5 May 1936 Italian troops entered Addis Ababa, the Abyssinian capital.

In June 1936 NEVILLE CHAMBERLAIN, then Chancellor of the Exchequer, said:

There is no reason why, because the policy of collective security, in the circumstances in which it was tried, has failed we should, therefore, abandon the idea of the League and give up the ideals for which the League stands. But if we have retained any vestige of common sense, surely we must admit that we have tried to impose upon the League a task which was beyond its powers to fulfil. (Quoted by Chamberlain himself in the House of Commons, 24 March 1938.)

On 10 June 1936 Chamberlain said that the continuation of economic sanctions would be the 'very midsummer of madness', and on 15 June sanctions were lifted by Britain.

The importance of this failure to apply effective sanctions was twofold. The League became discredited as an instrument for preserving peace, and Germany was able to see something of the weakness of democratic resolve and procedure.

ANTHONY EDEN wrote in his memoirs:

I had no doubt that [Hitler] was watching the Abyssinian struggle through all its phases and that he had taken heart from our failure to bring Mussolini to book. (*Memoirs*, p. 330.)

Other commentators agreed that the League's influence was over. LEO AMERY headed his chapter on Abyssinia in *My Political Life*— 'Killing the League'.

MAJOR-GENERAL TEMPERLEY wrote to Lord Allen of Hurtwood on 6 February 1936:

No one questions what the Covenant was intended to mean. The more practical issue is how our Government and public opinion will now interpret it. I am confident that no foreign Government, at this stage, would accept the obligations. Nor would our own people tolerate a firm obligation to fight for Danzig or Austria etc. At least I don't think so. (Unpublished letter, Allen Papers.)

LORD LOTHIAN wrote to Lloyd George on 23 May 1936:

I am sure that the League are wrong. And I am sure that you would make a mistake to identify yourself with them. Though they do not know it, they are simply playing the French anti-German game. All this stuff about collective security is simply 'encirclement' in a new form. . . .

We have got the game in our hands, but only if we refuse to join the 'encirclement' camp. If we rejoin the Stresa camp and undertake to keep Germany down, not only does it mean ultimate world war, but another free hand for Mussolini—to take Egypt and the Sudan in due time.

The collective security business—i.e. going to war to preserve a *status quo* you cannot change—is going to die a natural death in a few months. British common sense is going to kill it. (Unpublished letter; Lothian Papers.)

In March 1936 SIR ARNOLD WILSON wrote:

Of the fifty-seven varieties of States constituting the League, half are unfit for membership, for they cannot usefully assist its deliberations and cannot take responsibility for its decisions. It is no reflection on three negro or negroid states, three United States protectorates . . . and twenty South and Central American Republics to say that they are not a source of strength and do not make up for the absence of Japan, Germany, Brazil, U.S.A. and Egypt. . . .

If the League is to continue to exist the Covenant must, I submit, be altered in respect of Article XVI without delay. If this is impossible—and it may prove so—we should take the lead, with the concurrence of the Dominions and India, in declaring our intention to restrict its activities and to conduct serious and urgent international negotiations elsewhere . . . public opinion in this country will not tolerate, and would eject from office, a government which took sides in current international disputes in conformity with the Covenant. (*Walks and Talks Abroad*, pp. 273, 274.)

On 18 June 1936, LLOYD GEORGE said in the House of Commons:

'I have been in this House very nearly half a century. . . . I have never before heard a British Minister, speaking on behalf of the Government . . . say that Britain was beaten—Britain and her Empire beaten—and that we must abandon the enterprise we had taken in hand.'

He quoted the Prime Minister's message to the Peace Society, 'Let your aim be resolute, and your footsteps firm and certain.' And he went on:

'Here is the resolute aim; here is the certain footstep—*running away*! . . .

'The Right Hon. Gentleman has boasted today and he boasted in the last speech of his that I heard in the House, that we led the nations. That increased our responsibility. We led in the imposition of sanctions; we led also in the denunciation of the aggressor. We led, too, in proposing, I think, oil sanctions in principle; and we also led in selling oil in practice.'

LLOYD GEORGE turned to Neville Chamberlain and quoted Chamberlain's words at the last General Election:

'The choice before us is whether we shall make a last effort at Geneva for peace and security, or whether by a cowardly surrender we shall break all the promises we have made and hold ourselves up to the shame of our children and their children's children.'

Pointing to Stanley Baldwin, and those who sat next to him on the Government Front Bench, Lloyd George cried in a voice of scorn: 'Tonight, we have had the cowardly surrender, and *THERE* are the cowards!' (*Hansard*.)

On 31 July 1936 LEO AMERY told the House of Commons:

The fact is that in Europe today certain Powers, Germany for one and Italy for another, do not accept the theory, which finds favour with

Hon. Members opposite, of a League based upon coercion. If we stand by that conception, our League will, in fact, become an Anglo-Franco-Soviet alliance against Germany, Japan and Italy. That would be the worst situation which I could imagine in foreign politics, and one which might well make war inevitable. (*Hansard.*)

On 3 September ALFRED ZIMMERN wrote:

The point is to get the ordinary man to understand that the Wilsonian idea is more important than the misused Geneva instrument. . . . That is the foundation on which we must build our long distance policy. The plain man will not, and ought not to be asked to believe in a League composed partly of states who have destroyed the Rule of Law within their own borders. The 1920 League has too many 'passengers' from the beginning. (Unpublished letter, Allen Papers.)

On 20 February 1938 Anthony Eden resigned from the Foreign Secretaryship. WINSTON CHURCHILL told the House of Commons on 21 February:

The resignation of the late Foreign Secretary may well be a milestone in history. Great quarrels, it has been well said, arise from small occasions but seldom from small causes. The late Foreign Secretary adhered to the old policy which we have all forgotten for so long. The Prime Minister and his colleagues have entered upon another and a new policy. The old policy was an effort to establish the rule of law in Europe, and build up through the League of Nations effective deterrents against the aggressor. Is it the new policy to come to terms with the totalitarian Powers in the hope that by great and far-reaching acts of submission, not merely in sentiment and pride, but in material factors, peace may be preserved?

The other day Lord Halifax said that Europe was confused. The part of Europe which is confused is that part ruled by Parliamentary Governments. I know of no confusion on the side of the great Dictators. They know what they want, and no one can deny that up to the present at every step they are getting what they want. The grave and largely irreparable injury to world security took place in the years 1932 to 1935. (*Hansard.*)

German ambitions to annex Austria had become clear, but the League could not rouse itself to resist German action.

On 7 March 1938 NEVILLE CHAMBERLAIN told the House of Commons:

The League today is mutilated; it is halt and maimed. (*Hansard.*)

CLEMENT ATTLEE spoke in the House of Commons on 14 March 1938:

I do not think that you can settle the difficulties and dangers of the world by bargainings between one big Power and another. You can only do it by trying to establish, within the League, something like justice . . . I say today that, faced with this violent action in Austria, our reply should be, 'Back to League principles; back to the support of the rule of law' as the only way to maintain peace. (*Hansard.*)

WINSTON CHURCHILL also spoke:

If a number of States were assembled around Great Britain and France in a solemn treaty for mutual defence against aggression; if they had their forces marshalled in what you may call a grand alliance; if they had their staff arrangements concerted; if all this rested, as it can honourably rest, upon the Covenant of the League of Nations, agreeable with all the purposes and ideals of the League of Nations; if that were sustained, as it would be, by the moral sense of the world; and if it were done in the year 1938—and, believe me, it may be the last chance there will be for doing it—then I say that you might even now arrest this approaching war . . .

Before we cast away this hope, this cause, this plan, which I do not at all disguise has an element of risk, let those who wish to reject it ponder well and earnestly upon what will happen to us if, when all else has been thrown to the wolves, we are left to face our fate alone. (*Hansard.*)

In 1938 Germany demanded the annexation of the Sudeten area of Czechoslovakia, whose inhabitants were German speaking: former subjects of the Austro-Hungarian Empire. Britain intervened in the German–Czech crisis, and contributed towards persuading Czechoslovakia to allow Germany to annex the Sudeten areas. The League was not consulted. The Munich Agreement, whereby the conditions of the German annexation were fixed, was conducted far from League channels. Nor was League approval considered of any importance after Munich. By its failure to save Abyssinia from Mussolini, the League had become discredited. International forums were considered unnecessary. Bilateral agreements were regarded as better instruments of security than multilateral League resolutions.

In February 1939 Neville Chamberlain announced that Britain would come to the aid of France if France were attacked. On 9 February 1939 LORD ROBERT CECIL wrote to Gilbert Murray:

I am quite in favour of giving Neville's pledge to France, but honestly it is not a solution. It is only an emergency measure. I suppose the idea is to construct some kind of Peace bloc, and then from the Peace bloc to work back to something like the League. But though you may call it a Peace bloc, it is in fact only a counter-alliance called by another name, and I have never believed that alliances and armaments are any real solution of the international position. What hypocrisy it is now for the Government to go on saying they can do nothing with the League without Italy and Germany, when they are ready to face those two Powers in a defensive alliance with France alone! (Unpublished letter, Gilbert Murray Papers.)

On 21 February NEVILLE CHAMBERLAIN spoke in the House of Commons:

. . . the only chance that the League has of becoming again an effective factor in the preservation of peace will be when it has abandoned the idea that peace can be imposed by force. (*Hansard.*)

WINSTON CHURCHILL defended the collective use of force:

. . . It was the National Government who adopted these principles and popularised them, gathered to them the whole force of the country, and fought the election upon them. The Government's General Election manifesto contains this sentence. . . . 'The League of Nations will remain, as heretofore, the keystone of British policy.' (*Hansard.*)

On 31 March Chamberlain announced in the House of Commons that Britain had given Poland a unilateral guarantee against aggression.

GILBERT MURRAY wrote privately on 3 April:

If the League is dropped, I see grave dangers of the agreement with Poland becoming a mere military alliance on the balance of power principle. I mean, differences will be settled not by any attempt at impartial third-party judgment, but by a struggle based on power between the parties concerned. (Unpublished letter, Gilbert Murray Papers.)

LORD HALIFAX told the League on 23 May 1939:

We have, in consequence of what has passed, felt obliged to undertake certain obligations of a peculiar character directed towards pacific and well-defined ends. One principle is common to all those obligations which we have assumed—namely, resistance to the imposition of solutions by the method of force, which, if continued, must result in reducing civilisation to anarchy and destruction.

The particular action which His Majesty's Government has taken has not been carried out through the League. This was, in the circumstances, impossible. But everything that His Majesty's Government has done is in strict conformity with the spirit of the League Covenant. (*League of Nations Official Journal*, May–June 1939, pp. 364–5.)

On 1 September 1939 Germany attacked Poland, and two days later Britain and France declared war on Germany.

A member of the League of Nations Union, R. A. F. S. ROBERTSON, wrote on 8 October, to Gilbert Murray:

Do you not think that the League of Nations ought to have been summoned when Poland was attacked by Germany? Surely indeed it ought also to have been summoned when Herr Hitler committed an act of Aggression in Bohemia last September? Ought it not even now to be summoned in order that a powerful statement of our Case and Aims might be presented to the World? (Unpublished letter, Murray Papers.)

The League was at last summoned, not to judge Germany for her occupation of Prague, or for her invasion of Warsaw, but to expel Russia, who had invaded Finland in November.

GILBERT MURRAY wrote privately on 23 December 1939:

The Assembly seemed to me encouraging, the rapidity and spontaneity with which it has assembled was quite striking, and the main feeling in the atmosphere was unmistakeable, the worm turning at last against these repeated violations of the Covenant. (Unpublished letter, Gilbert Murray Papers.)

On 14 December 1939 the League Council expelled Russia from the League.

R. A. BUTLER spoke for Britain, voting for Russia's expulsion:

The movement of world opinion, the moral and material support which has been given to the Finnish cause, is due in large measure to sympathy and admiration for the Finnish nation. But the strength of the general feeling in the world derives also from the realisation that another blow is being struck at the foundations on which the existence of all of us as independent nations is founded. It appears to us a blow not only against our independency but against those national institutions which we have so patiently evolved within our boundaries. Wild movements have been loosed which seem to threaten the life of free peoples. . . .

. . . the principles of the Covenant remain and their observance is in the best interests of international society. We do not cling to them out of some old-fashioned belief or desire that the world should never be changed; we adhere to them because they form the best and only inspiration upon which an international order can be based. These principles are now being challenged, and the challenge gives us the opportunity to prove their worth. It will be our duty, in our generation, to make the principles which invite us here prevail. (*League of Nations Official Journal*, November–December 1939, pp. 505–8.)

France

During the Paris Peace Conference, Britain and America proposed to guarantee France against German aggressions. LORD ESHER wrote to a friend on 7 April 1919:

I am sorry for the French and I understand them well. They are a realistic people and not given to Anglo-Saxon idealism. The choice appears to be, between material guarantees that their population of thirty-five millions is not a prey to eighty-five millions of Germans, and guarantees from England and America which are not likely to be and perhaps cannot be given. (*Journals and Letters*, p. 228.)

WINSTON CHURCHILL commented:

Worn down, doubly decimated, but undisputed masters of the hour, the French nation peered into the future in thankful wonder and haunting dread. Where then was that SECURITY without which all that had been gained seemed valueless, and life itself, even amid the rejoicings of victory, was almost unendurable? The mortal need was Security at all costs and by all methods, however stern or even harsh. (*The Gathering Storm*, p. 5.)

The House of Commons debated the Anglo–French Treaty at 2.50 a.m. in the early hours of 22 July 1919. LLOYD GEORGE said:

I do not believe that a man would hesitate to go to the aid of France if she were attacked. I was talking to a very prominent . . . rather an extreme Socialist. I said to him, 'We are going to give an undertaking that if France is attacked Great Britain will come to her assistance.' He said, 'I do not believe there is a man in the British Islands who would object to that.' (*Hansard*.)

LIEUT.-COMMANDER KENWORTHY followed:

Unfortunately, there are men in France in high stations who follow the rules of the Bourbon rulers, and one of the things they have not forgotten is that this system of alliances does not prevent war, but leads to war. . . . Why should France especially have this reinsurance when Germany is down and out, to use the language of the boxing ring? . . .

I think that if France is to have it [others] ought to have it . . . Italy . . .
the new State of Czechoslovakia, and every one of the new States and
the old. I would like to have seen a general reinsurance for all nations. . . .
Here we have the three aristocratic nations of the world—the English,
French and Americans, perpetrating a blunder which kills the League
of Nations at its birth. (*Hansard.*)

On 19 November 1919 the American Senate rejected the Versailles
Treaty, and this vote was confirmed and finalised on 19 March 1920.
ARNOLD TOYNBEE pointed out the effect on France of America's
action:

Thus the Franco–American agreement was never ratified; the exchange of ratifications of the Franco–British agreement remained without effect . . . and France found herself in an extraordinarily difficult
and harassing position, which determined her state of mind, and
consequently her policy, during the years which followed. As the
invaded country in which the most intense and the most devastating
actions had been fought in a military struggle which had focused the
destructive energies of Mankind upon French soil, France had been the
principal victim of the War. Her richest territories had been laid waste
and the already serious decline in her birth-rate had been alarmingly
accelerated. . . . In this perplexing condition of uncertain strength and
latent weakness she was left by her late Allies and Associates in the
West to maintain against Germany . . . a new map of Europe which
she could never have brought into existence single-handed. (*Survey of
International Affairs 1920–23*, p. 59.)

On 8 August 1919 the German Government was allowed by Britain
and France to send 17,000 troops into the demilitarised Right Bank of
the Rhine, where civil government was threatened by revolutionary
uprisings. On 19 March 1920 Germany asked permission to send in
more than 17,000. France opposed this; Britain favoured it. Before a
decision was reached, on 3 April 1920, Germany sent in 20,000 troops.
France, claiming a breach of the Treaty, at once occupied Frankfort
and Darmstadt. Britain had not agreed to this. AUSTEN CHAMBERLAIN
wrote, in January 1920:

She [France] went in against the expressed sense of every Ally and
America, used black troops to occupy Frankfort, and might easily
have provoked serious trouble. I think Millerand and Poincaré with
Foch to egg them on very dangerous, and it was time to let them know
that if they provoked or provoke a row by isolated action, they will be

left to settle it by themselves as best they can. They live in a nightmare terror of Germany, but unless they are careful they will plant such memories as Germany will never forget, and someday will avenge. (*The Life and Letters of Austen Chamberlain*, p. 155.)

LORD ROBERT CECIL told the House of Commons on 25 May 1922:

I think any breach of our *Entente* with France would be a real disaster to Europe. I do not mean by that that we should always conform in policy to French policy. We must have our own policy and must carry it out. If French policy is, in the opinion of our Government, leading towards war that would be too great a price to pay even to avoid a shaking of the *Entente*, but do not let us underrate the grave disadvantage of a breach with France. (*Hansard.*)

The French wished to enforce German reparations payments. Lloyd George urged moderation. But the quarrel between France and Britain was bitter and prolonged. LLOYD GEORGE said in the House of Commons on 31 May 1922:

We have stood for a policy of moderation and restraint. We have stood for the policy of considering the difficulties of Germany, and in doing so we have rendered ourselves liable to a good deal of misrepresentation between France and ourselves. (*Hansard.*)

LORD ROBERT CECIL replied:

It would be much better for the Government to make up their minds definitely what their policy in the matter is and to go quite freely and candidly to the French and say, 'We have arrived at the conclusion that we did try to get too much out of Germany. . . . Let us agree to a more moderate policy.' . . .

Frankness and openness will restore, much more rapidly than any skilled wizardry, good relations between the two countries. (*Hansard.*)

Hostility to France was widespread. J. M. KEYNES wrote in 1922:

I hope that France will abandon her opposition to proposals for reduced military and naval establishments. What a handicap her youth will suffer if she maintains conscription whilst her neighbours, voluntarily or involuntarily, have abandoned it! . . .

I hope too, that France will forget her dangerous ambitions in Central Europe and will limit strictly those in the Near East; for both are based on rubbishy foundations and will bring her no good. That she has anything to fear from Germany in the future which we can foresee, except what she may herself provoke, is a delusion. . . . Germany's future now lies to the East. . . . (*A Revision of the Treaty*, p. 186.)

On 14 November 1922 Germany sought a moratorium on reparations for three or four years. On 9 December 1922 the London Conference considered this request. The French refused a moratorium, claiming that Germany was already a defaulter on payments and threatened to occupy the Ruhr if Germany failed to meet France's demands. GEORGE V wrote, in January 1923:

I consider the French will make a grave error if they go into the Ruhr. By doing so they will make Germany bankrupt and turn her bolshevik and throw her into the arms of Russia. (*King George V*, p. 373.)

The French did occupy the Ruhr; Anglo–French relations became extremely strained, and when France withdrew her troops Britain was delighted. But Austen Chamberlain saw the folly of an Anglo–French quarrel, and sought, by the Locarno Treaty, to satisfy France and Germany.

LORD D'ABERNON, British Ambassador to Berlin from 1920 to 1926, commented on the proposed Locarno Treaty on 3 October 1925:

From being an ex-enemy, Germany becomes a Power with equal rights, whose frontiers will be guaranteed by a Treaty, the Treaty guaranteed by England. Thus, both Germany and France have this security for the safety of their frontiers—that aggression brings in England against the aggressor.

As regards England, it may be said that we take a risk. . . . But this guarantee is the best means of preventing aggression. (*An Ambassador of Peace*, vol. 3, p. 193.)

On 16 October 1925 the Locarno Agreement was signed, the Governments concerned stating 'that the entry into force of these treaties and conventions will contribute greatly to bring about a moral relaxation of the tension between nations. . .'. Annex A of the Agreement was a *Treaty of Mutual Guarantee between Germany, Belgium, France, Great Britain and Italy*.

Article 2 began:

Germany and Belgium, and also Germany and France, mutually undertake that they will in no case attack or invade each other or resort to war against each other. . . .

Article 4 contained the sentence:

In case of a flagrant violation of Article 2 . . . by one of the high contracting parties, each of the other contracting parties undertakes immediately to come to the help of the party against whom such a violation or breach has been directed. . . .

The Locarno agreements, of which there were five, involved Germany, Belgium, France, Great Britain, Italy, Poland and Czechoslovakia. Austen Chamberlain signed for Britain, Mussolini for Italy.

Article 1 of the *Treaty of Mutual Guarantee* reaffirmed the Rhineland clauses of the Treaty of Versailles. The text of the Locarno agreements is given in D'Abernon, *An Ambassador of Peace*, vol. 3, Appendix V.

ANTHONY EDEN wrote in retrospect:

Austen Chamberlain, in appearance and sometimes in speech, could be stiff and forbidding. This had nothing to do with the real man, who was warm-hearted, considerate and generous. He was incapable of a mean action and conscientious to a fault. . . . Sir Austen's international policies were based on a traditional Foreign Office pattern. They were none the worse for that. A francophile, he was once ridiculed for observing that he loved France as a woman, for her defects as well as for her qualities. But he was wise to found his efforts to pacify Europe on Anglo–French unity. With the help of the confidence thus created Germany was brought into the Locarno Treaty. . . . By the same process of thought, he accepted the significance of the Little Entente and was a friend of their statesmen, believing also that, while the Hapsburg Empire could not be revived, Austrian independence must be defended. Had he lived, I have little doubt what his reactions must have been to his half-brother Neville's Central European policies; for him the fate of Czechoslovakia could never be 'because of a quarrel in a faraway country between a people of whom we know nothing'. (*Facing the Dictators*, p. 7.)

The House of Commons debated the Locarno Treaty on 18 November 1925.

AUSTEN CHAMBERLAIN said:

. . . the agreements made at Locarno, valuable as they are in themselves—and I beg the House not to under-rate their intrinsic value—are yet more valuable for the spirit which produced them. . . . We regard Locarno, not as the end of the work of appeasement and reconciliation, but as its beginning. . . .

I had not met representatives of the German Empire until I met them at that Conference. I very soon was able to satisfy myself that they came there animated by the same sincere desire for peace and reconciliation that animated the Western nations. (*Hansard*.)

LLOYD GEORGE said:

France, on her part, was getting a guarantee from the greatest Empire in the world for the security of her frontiers, and, so far as Germany was concerned, it was a voluntary acceptance by her statesmen of the frontiers of defeat. That was a very great act of courage. (*Hansard*.)

LORD LONDONDERRY wrote in 1938:

Although it marked a great step forward on the road to collective security, the Treaty of Locarno contained serious defects. In the first place it was capable, and theoretically still is capable, of involving us in serious complications with Germany. For instance, by virtue of our guaranteeing the Franco–German frontier we might quite well be required to come to the support of France, even if she had, by a provocative policy, exposed her territory to an attack which might be more in the nature of a counter-offensive than an act of aggression. . . . Again, the incorporation of the 'Rhineland clauses' from the Versailles Treaty, and the absence in the Locarno Agreement of any provision for their modification or ultimate cancellation was a one-sided as well as short-sighted arrangement. Sooner or later it was bound to constitute a grievance which Germany would refuse to tolerate, as indeed many foretold at the time. (*Ourselves and Germany*, p. 35.)

A. P. HERBERT wrote a poem entitled:

FOREIGN POLICY; OR, THE UNIVERSAL AUNT

The foreigner's an alien,
He does not rule the waves;
Give me the good Australian
Who cleans his teeth and shaves.
Oh, let the hairy Magyar
Stew in his horrid juice,
And scrap the Foreign Office,
For it ain't no kind of use!

Poor old Britannier! Talk about disarm?
It's these here diplomatists that do the greatest harm.

45

Scrap the Foreign Office! Why d'you want to roam?
Ain't you got enough misfortunes in the home?

> The paper's all Croatians
>   And Jugo-Slavs and Czechs,
> In all these bearded nations
>   We're buried to the necks;
> But it takes a flood or earthquake
>   Or other nasty mess
> To get the British Empire
>   Into the British Press!

Poor old Britannier! Excuse a little sob;
Ain't your far-flung Empire a whole-time job?
Less of this Locarny-blarney! Why d'you want to roam?
Ain't you got enough misfortunes in the home?

(*A Book of Ballads*, pp. 406–7.)

France stood firmest of the Allied Powers in demanding reparations payments from Germany to the extent that Englishmen regarded reparations as harsh, so France was seen as being unduly severe. LLOYD GEORGE was quite convinced that France was in the wrong, not only economically (for he thought that the end of reparations would be the beginning of prosperity), but morally:

It may be added that France is the last country that should stand on a punctilio about the Treaty of Versailles. What about armaments; and the pledge implicit in the Treaty that German disarmament should be followed and paralleled by her own? Yet France has today an army, with reserves, of over five million, and thousands of heavy guns. . . . The immense land armaments of France are a glaring and arrogant breach of the undertakings of Versailles. (*The Truth about Reparations and War Debts*, p. 139.)

WINSTON CHURCHILL, speaking at Chingford in Essex on 13 November 1933, said:

I am a friend of France. They are a peace-loving people. They have no ambitions to fulfil except to defend their own country. They are satisfied with things as they are.

I am sure they were right in 1914. Everything that has happened in these last few years proves the German War Guilt and the dangerous character of the German people when dominated by autocratic Government.

Therefore I have been for more than 20 years a consistent friend of France and a consistent opponent of the German danger. (The *Manchester Guardian*, 14 November 1933.)

Locarno had brought France and England close together, and Aristide Briand, who was in charge of French foreign policy for all but one day from 1925 to 1932, worked in the same neighbourly spirit as had Austen Chamberlain. But in 1933 Adolf Hitler came to power in Germany and sought to make Germany powerful. He turned to Britain for help; and the lingering hostility to France helped him in his overtures. Britain recognised the inequality of an unarmed Germany, and neglected to consider whether France might not regard German weakness as a security. Germany asked for a larger Navy, and Britain accepted this request, without consulting France. On 18 June 1935 the Anglo–German Naval Agreement was signed. It shook French confidence in Britain, and strengthened Pierre Laval's argument that France must herself seek an understanding with Germany.

On 5 July 1935 SIR ROBERT VANSITTART wrote:

We have let National Defence run down. . . . This would perhaps have been dangerous in any case. It becomes far more dangerous if we are to alienate all our prospective friends and allies as well, those in fact who have felt themselves hitherto in one boat. This alienation has, of late years, been largely influenced by the desire to placate Germany. In reason that is well. But beyond reason—and it goes beyond reason in some quarters, including ministerial quarters—the pursuit of a jack-o-lantern will land us irretrievably in a bog. (See biography of Lord Vansittart by Ian Colvin.)

Encouraged, perhaps, by the Anglo–German Naval Agreement and convinced that Britain would not support France in a Franco–German quarrel, Hitler sent his troops into the Rhineland. Under the Versailles Treaty the Rhineland was to be a demilitarised zone, to safeguard France from attack. The Locarno Agreement had reaffirmed the demilitarisation. But as ANTHONY EDEN pointed out in his memoirs:

There was a flaw in the Locarno Treaty of which both we and the French were conscious. The Locarno powers would not resort to war unless first attacked or in the event of a flagrant breach of the demilitarized zone. 'Flagrant' was not defined, but it was taken for granted that the sending of troops into the Rhineland would be an immediate prelude to an attack on France and Belgium. Hitler cleverly exploited this ambiguity. As there was no sign of any German intention to attack

France, he argued that his action was not a 'flagrant breach' of the Treaty. The British public had become so accustomed to thinking of Locarno as a guarantee against a repetition of what happened in 1914, and not as a guarantee of the demilitarized zone that, when there was no German attack on France or Belgium, they saw no cause for alarm. Even the French, who are more legalistically minded than us, seem to have doubts whether, on this occasion, the Locarno guarantee came instantly into force and whether 'immediate action' was justified, when there was no actual attack to be repelled. All this did not in my eyes seriously minimize the gravity of the Nazi deed, but it confused the event. (*Facing the Dictators*.)

ANTHONY EDEN reported to the Cabinet:

The myth is now exploded that Herr Hitler only repudiates treaties imposed on Germany by force. We must be prepared for him to repudiate any treaty even if freely negotiated (*a*) when it becomes inconvenient, and (*b*) when Germany is sufficiently strong and the circumstances are otherwise favourable for doing so.

On the other hand, owing to Germany's growing material strength and power of mischief in Europe, it is in our interest to conclude with her as far-reaching and enduring a settlement as possible whilst Herr Hitler is in the mood to do so. But on entering upon this policy we must bear in mind that, whatever time-limits may be laid down in such a settlement, Herr Hitler's signature can only be considered as valid under the conditions specified above. (*Facing the Dictators*, p. 345.)

ANTHONY EDEN expressed a now widely held conviction when he wrote in 1962:

Hitler's occupation of the Rhineland was an occasion when the British and French Governments should have attempted the impossible. Academically speaking, there is little dispute that Hitler should have been called to order, if need be forcibly, at his first breach of an international agreement. But nobody was prepared to do it, in this country literally nobody; even the most warlike proclaimed that the League Council must be called, which would not have endorsed the use of force. . . . (*Facing the Dictators*, p. 366.)

The use of force on behalf of France was not so popular at the time. On 23 May 1936 THOMAS JONES told Stanley Baldwin:

We should not be compromised into undertaking to protect Austria from falling in the lap of Germany. We do not mean to fight for

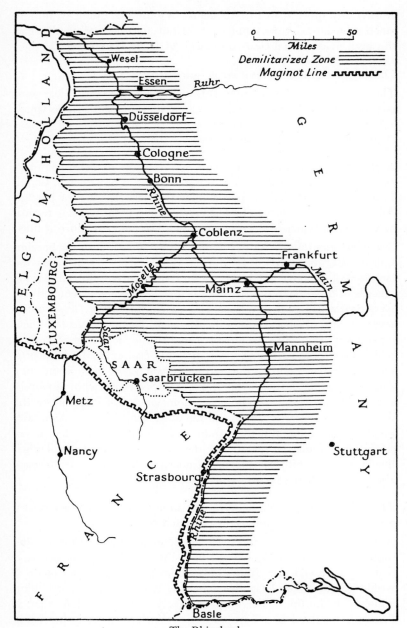

The Rhineland

Austria any more than for Abyssinia. We are not going to impose sanctions against Germany under any formula of collective security. Has this been made crystal clear to France? (*A Diary With Letters*, p. 208.)

On 23 July LORD LOTHIAN wrote to a friend:

The essence of the French folly is to try to get us to go to war with Germany when Germany is merely asking to be given the rights which are still regarded as the inherent rights of every sovereign nation. (Unpublished letter, Lothian Papers.)

Anthony Eden resigned as Foreign Secretary on 19 February 1938. Many of his critics had accused him of being too pro-French. On 24 February R. A. Butler, the new Under Secretary of State for Foreign Affairs, visited the German Embassy. According to the German record, R. A. BUTLER criticised Eden's pro-French bias, and explained it thus:

The generation of officials occupying the key positions in the Foreign Office today had grown up during a time when French was the language of diplomacy. For this reason it necessarily followed that the officials of the foreign service, both before and after they entered this service, attached, and were forced to attach, importance to spending several years in France to study the language. The result was that these officials very frequently acquired a biased attitude in favour of France, which they always retained, even after they had gradually been promoted to higher positions during the postwar years. In addition, they had obtained in Eden a young Foreign Secretary who obviously shared this attitude. . . . The generation which had come up in the foreign service in recent years, on the other hand, was free from any pro-French leaning. But this group in the Foreign Office had never really made much headway, and the first real break in the French line had come with Sir Nevile Henderson. (*Documents on German Foreign Policy*, Series D, vol. I, no. 128.)

The pro-French politicians were in a minority. ROBERT BOOTHBY told the House of Commons on 14 March 1938:

Although we have not collective security in any concrete form at the moment . . . fortunately we still have the friendship of France, and that is a very concrete thing. This, at least, we must hold on to. I would go further and say that I believe it would have a stabilising influence in Europe if the Prime Minister were to reiterate that, if France is involved in a European quarrel which involves her being attacked, we shall go to her support with our armed forces at once.

On 24 March 1938 WINSTON CHURCHILL told the House of Commons:

Great Britain and France have to stand together for mutual protection. Why should not the conditions be worked out precisely and the broad facts made public? Everyone knows, for instance, that our Air Force is triple in deterrent effectiveness if it operates from French bases . . . the fact that an attack upon this country would bring the attacker into conflict with the French army is another great security to us here. We are obliged in return to go to the aid of France, and hitherto we have always been better than our word.

Here, then, is the great security for the two countries. Proclaim it. Do not conceal it. Proclaim it, implement it, work it out in thorough detail. Treat the defensive problems of the two countries as if they were one. Then you will have a great deterrent against unprovoked aggression, and if the deterrent fails to deter, you will have a highly organised method of coping with the aggressor. (*Hansard.*)

These two voices were almost alone.

GENERAL IRONSIDE wrote in his diary on 25 March 1938:

Winston Churchill argued . . . [for] an immediate and close military alliance with France. Personally, I cannot see that we could ally ourselves blindly with France. We have many common interests, but we have many which are not common. . . . They love order in their plans, [which] often become inhuman and impracticable in consequence. We cannot make hypothetical plans to meet uncertain circumstances. We are arch-improvisers. We hate jumping fences before there is any necessity. Our problems are so vague that we must keep our plans liquid. . . . (*The Ironside Diaries*, p. 51.)

The Czech crisis was solved by Britain and Germany acting together. Britain took it upon herself to urge the Czechs to make concessions to Germany. France was not invited to play a leading part in the crisis. She was only asked to confirm what Britain had decided already. Chamberlain went alone to Hitler to the two crucial meetings, and only invited France to the third, more formal conference at Munich.

On 7 February 1939 SIR A. LAMBERT WARD said in the House of Commons:

There is not the slightest doubt that Czechoslovakia was led astray, not by us but by our allies . . . if the Czech Government in the pre-Munich days had not thought that they would be entitled to support from both France and Russia, they would have come to an agreement with the Sudeten Germans which would have been very much more to their benefit . . . the Czech Government [were] encouraged to stand out by promises that were made largely by France. (*Hansard*.)

DUFF COOPER replied:

I had not intended to speak, and I do not think that unless . . . [Sir A. Lambert Ward] had intervened, I should have spoken. . . . He admitted that Czechoslovakia had been let down, and he attempted to shift all the blame upon the great friendly country, to which he referred inaccurately as our ally, France. . . . There is no truth whatever, I maintain, for the allegation that the Czecho-Slovak Government were encouraged during the summer and autumn of last year to maintain an intransigent attitude by the French. . . . If wrong was done at Munich it was done by France and England together, and if blame is to be borne we should not seek to shirk our share of it. (*Hansard*.)

When Hitler threatened Poland in August 1939 Britain and France had still not fallen into the habit of easy or quick collaboration. Both hoped that Poland would make concessions to Germany and thus avoid war. Both asked Mussolini to urge Hitler to hold his hand. Neither told the other of these plans. When Germany invaded Poland both still sought delay and expected compromise. France delayed her declaration of war even longer than Britain. Perhaps Munich taught France that the initiative no longer lay with her. Britain was certainly prepared to negotiate with Hitler, or with Mussolini, without consulting France: the 'spirit' of the 1935 Anglo–German Naval Agreement persisted until 1939.

G. R. G. MURE wrote to Lord Vansittart in June 1943:

So far as I can judge, it never even occurs to ninety per cent of the public that any of the blame for the fall of France rests on us. The psychological self-adjustment of this country in June 1940 was a quite staggering phenomenon. We told ourselves that France had gone rotten and let us down, but that it was really rather a good thing to have no allies to consult: it made one so unhampered and independent. We congratulated ourselves on having scrupulously fulfilled all our obligations to France since September '39, and clean shut our minds (not that they were ever very wide open) to the history of the previous twenty years.

Now we flatter ourselves that for a year we stood alone which, whatever the gallantry of Fighter Command and the just repute of the British Navy, was after all largely due to our geographical position. The French: we either despise or pity. It depends whether conceit or sentimentality dominates in us. I do not believe that one Englishman in a thousand feels any shame for the part his country played for twenty years in the collapse of France, or has even asked himself what the most fair-minded Frenchman is probably thinking about England. . . .

. . . Yet ought we not be made to recollect how we behaved towards France between '19 and '39? Whatever we do with Germany and Italy after the war, an appalling vacuum will be left in western Europe. If it is not partly filled by a reasonably friendly France, God help us. I do not see how this is going to be achieved without a public acknowledgement of our own mistakes.

Would you not agree that the time is coming when somebody should remind the British public rather sharply that the French always have known and do now know, the German for what he is a good deal better than we; that if Frenchmen grew cynical, corrupt, and disloyal to their own country, we by virtually ignoring our own responsibility for the protection of the world from Germany heavily manured the soil on which French defeatism and treason grew; . . . (Unpublished letter in author's possession.)

LORD VANSITTART replied on 22 June 1943:

. . . I feel that we certainly should develop the theme of the considerable percentage of our guilt over the ultimate downfall of France, and that that guilt began to run from the very conclusion of the Entente. Our insularity and blindness completely took the heart out of our allies. From the Anglo–French Agreement of 1904 onward we really became a continental Power, and most obstinately refused to face the fact or to act like one. It is a most discreditable period in our history, and a guilty conscience made this country all the more Francophobe. . . . (Unpublished letter in author's possession.)

Rearmament and Public Opinion

On 16 June 1919 GEORGES CLEMENCEAU, the French Prime Minister, wrote to Brockdorff-Rantzau:

The Allied and Associated Powers wish to make it clear that their requirements in regard to German armaments were not made solely with the object of rendering it impossible for Germany to resume her policy of military aggression. They are also the first steps towards that general reduction and limitation of armaments which they seek to bring about as one of the most fruitful preventives of war. (Quoted in *Diplomacy in Fetters*, by Victor Wellesley, p. 55.)

On 1 March 1921 WINSTON CHURCHILL, then Secretary of State for Air, explained why he opposed any serious reduction of the Air Estimates:

It is said . . . 'Is not the war over, was not the last war the war to end war? . . . Has it not put an end to all international rivalry, has it not led to general disarmament? . . .'
. . . when it comes to cutting in upon necessities . . . surely we should be committing a very great folly. . . .
In place of what you had lost there would no doubt be a gain. You would no doubt establish some very convenient and imposing air services . . . a limited number of persons who could afford to pay very high rates would be carried and would be able to cross the world at unprecedented speed. I should very much like to see that done . . . but to say that such results are comparable to the solid and indispensable work done by the Royal Air Force . . . to defend our country and our Empire is an absurdity. You would throw away the one essential of your life in order to adopt what is undoubtedly a great convenience and an advance in civilisation. . . . The story would not end there. A day would come when powerful nations, beginning to recover from the War, and to gather their power together again, would become the cause of rumours in this country. There would be rumours that in the heart of Germany or Russia there were great aerial developments of a very serious character, or of a character which might easily have a military complexion. Then you would have a war scare. (*Hansard*.)

On 18 November 1925 DUFF COOPER told the House of Commons:

I think that many of those who talk so much about disarmament and who are such sincere lovers of peace are approaching the question from the wrong end because they are seeking to obtain peace by disarmament instead of promoting that feeling of security which will lead to a policy of disarmament. (*Hansard.*)

On 4 December 1929 the House of Commons discussed whether it was desirable 'that His Majesty's Government should use its utmost efforts to stimulate international action for the study and eventual preparation' of an armaments limitation treaty. LLOYD GEORGE pointed out:

The time will come when it will be noted that this Debate on a subject upon which future civilisation may depend is being conducted in practically an empty House. . . .

We disarmed Germany. . . . We destroyed millions of her rifles, her cannon, her aeroplanes; and we sank many of her ships; and we have not yet begun to carry out our part of the Treaty of Versailles. . . .

You are not going to get peace with thirty millions of armed men and gigantic armaments. The chariot of peace cannot advance along a road cluttered with cannon. (*Hansard.*)

The League of Nations took up the task of bringing about General Disarmament by Treaty; and many people were prepared to judge the effectiveness or otherwise of the League by its achievements at the Disarmament Conference.

LORD LONDONDERRY wrote:

It was my duty to serve throughout as one of the British delegates to the Disarmament Conference.

Mr Arthur Henderson, who was the Chairman of that Conference, undertook his work though a very sick and ailing man with a courage which all must admire, but in my judgment he missed a great opportunity. Perhaps his failing health prevented him from taking the leading part in the early stages of the Conference, which lacked from the beginning the powerful influence of a leader to co-ordinate its activities and to insist on a statement as early as possible of a practical nature. Instead of that, Committees with vague terms of reference pursued interminable discussions, most of them on completely theoretical lines with the result that the Disarmament Conference languished and died unmourned and unsung, with nothing whatsoever of a constructive nature which could possibly be placed to its credit. (*Ourselves and Germany*, p. 47.)

LORD LONDONDERRY wrote to his wife on 17 July 1932:

. . . We are having a difficult task here and everything goes to show how inopportune a Disarmament Conference is. It gives all the little States the opportunity of condemning all weapons because they have no responsibilities except local ones, and weapons in their hands are quite useless. The Great Powers have manifold responsibilities all over the world, and it is foolish to pretend that the authority of the Great Powers can be made to depend by a stroke of the pen on moral influences rather than on an adequate element of force. (*Ourselves and Germany*, pp. 47–8.)

LORD LONDONDERRY concluded:

As total disarmament was obviously out of the question, no country could assume that, if it divested itself of all weapons of defence, it could attain that measure of security which every nation has the right to demand of its rulers, but in the practical, simple policy of limitation of armaments, I am quite convinced the problem of disarmament was capable of solution. The British Draft Convention was a practical proposal and was put forward by Mr Ramsay MacDonald; unfortunately, it received very little support, and died a natural death. Again, this was due to the attitude of France, who was unwilling to concede to Germany that equality which would have constituted her the partner in the task of the settlement of the world. (*Ourselves and Germany*, p. 48.)

The Germans pointed out that while they had accepted the terms of the Versailles Treaty and disarmed, France had not. Before accepting a General Disarmament Treaty, they insisted upon the right to increase their own armaments to the French level. On 10 November 1932 GEORGE LANSBURY told the House of Commons:

The nations of Europe have performed a great disservice to the German nation by not following their pledged word and disarming themselves when they had disarmed Germany. . . .

We talk about scraps of paper, but this supposed Peace Treaty, signed between the Great Powers and Germany, has never been honoured, and the result is that Germany has got sick with hope deferred. (*Hansard.*)

On 23 November 1932 WINSTON CHURCHILL said in the House of Commons:

... the demand is that Germany should be allowed to rearm. Do not delude yourselves. Do not let His Majesty's Government believe, I am sure they do not believe, that all that Germany is asking for is equal status. I believe the refined term now is equal qualitative status, or, as an alternative, equal quantative status by indefinitely deferred stages. This is not what Germany is seeking. All these bands of sturdy Teutonic youths, marching along the streets and roads of Germany, with the light in their eyes of desire to suffer for their Fatherland, are not looking for status. They are looking for weapons, and, when they have the weapons, believe me they will then ask for the return, the restoration of lost territories and lost colonies. (*Hansard*.)

LEO AMERY spoke in the same debate:

The trouble is that the Governments of the world have consistently shirked the real issues and have played about with the sham issue of disarmament. It was so much easier with disarmament to say: 'This is a matter for a Preparatory Commission, and then for another Preparatory Commission', in the hope that the thing might be postponed indefinitely. . . .

 . . . meanwhile the Governments of Europe—they are responsible, and our successive Governments have been equally responsible—have built up a Frankenstein monster in the shape of a sincere, well-meaning, unintelligent public opinion, hypnotised by the continued identification of disarmaments with peace. . . .

'The prophets prophesy falsely, and the priests bear rule by these means; and my people love to have it so; and what will ye do in the end thereof?' (*Hansard*.)

The Disarmament Conference continued into 1933. There was some chance that it might succeed. A Draft Convention was drawn up, and Anthony Eden was sent to Geneva to bring negotiations to a successful conclusion. But events in Germany prevented this. Adolf Hitler came to power, and his interest in Disarmament was small. The German delegate began to hinder negotiations.

Writing to Baldwin on 1 May 1933, ANTHONY EDEN said:

I only wish we had more to show in the way of results. The Germans are exasperating and progress is very slow. One feels it is rather like a 1917 campaign in Flanders; we can only make such progress as we may in the mud between the pill-boxes and leave the strong points to be attacked at the last—and as in Flanders, the pill-boxes are occupied by Germans. . . .

This job is like trying to force a bill through an international House of Commons with no whips and no governing majority. (*Facing the Dictators*, p. 37.)

The Nazis insisted on equality of arms with France as a pre-condition to any Disarmament Treaty. In England Sir John Simon appeared to support their claim. So did Lord Lothian, who regarded a disarmed Germany as one of the bad legacies of Versailles, and who saw no security as far as Europe was concerned in a weak Germany bordering upon a strong France.

The Disarmament Conference might have gone on for ever; France had no intention of allowing Germany to rearm. Instead, Germany left the Conference, and, with her departure, its effective deliberations came to an abrupt end.

On 25 October 1933 John Wilmot, the Labour candidate at East Fulham, defeated his Conservative opponent. The seat had been held by the Conservatives with a majority of 3,000 votes; John Wilmot obtained a 7,000 majority—a turnover of 10,000 votes.

HUGH DALTON, who canvassed for Wilmot, wrote:

John Wilmot owed the size of his majority to four factors; first, to his advocacy, not of 'pacifism', but of collective defence through a strong League of Nations and a General Disarmament Treaty, and to his most effective exposure of the shameful slackness and obstructive incompetence of the British Government in Geneva; second, to his equally effective exposure of bad local housing conditions . . . third, to the superiority of his electoral organisation . . . fourth, and not least, to his own personality and outstanding political ability. (*Hitler's War: Before and After*, pp. 58–60.)

It was suggested, however, that Labour won East Fulham solely on a 'pacifist' vote; and the lesson was drawn—erroneously perhaps—that 'the electorate of England' demanded a pacifist policy. Although East Fulham was a shock to the Conservatives, it must be remembered that it only reduced their numbers from 551 to 550—an absolute majority *after* East Fulham of 488. Yet Baldwin interpreted East Fulham as a warning that he himself ought to pursue a 'pacifist' policy.

On 12 November 1936 STANLEY BALDWIN told the House of Commons:

You will remember the election at Fulham in the autumn of 1933, when a seat which the National Government held was lost by 7,000 votes on no issue but the pacifist. . . . My position as the leader of a great party was not altogether a comfortable one . . . supposing I had gone to the country and said that Germany was rearming and that we must rearm, does anybody think that this pacifist democracy would have rallied to that cry at that moment? I cannot think of anything that would have made the loss of the election from my point of view more certain. (*Hansard.*)

It was this speech which occasioned Winston Churchill's reference, in the index to *The Gathering Storm*: 'Baldwin . . . confesses putting party before country.'

Of the East Fulham by-election WINSTON CHURCHILL remarked in retrospect:

It would be wrong in judging the policy of the British Government not to remember the passionate desire for peace which animated the uninformed, misinformed majority of the British people, and seemed to threaten with political extinction any party or politician who dared to take any other line. This, of course, is no excuse for political leaders who fall short of their duty. It is much better for parties or politicians to be turned out of office than to imperil the life of the nation. Moreover, there is no record in our history of any Government asking Parliament and the people for the necessary measures of defence and being refused. (*The Gathering Storm*, p. 104.)

During 1934 there was evidence that, contrary to Versailles, Germany was secretly rearming. France wanted to expose German wickedness, and take concerted action with Britain. On 30 April 1934 LORD ALLEN OF HURTWOOD wrote to a friend:

I incline to think it would be a mistake to seem to be on the side of France about the secret rearming of Germany under the *Versailles Treaty*. To do that means, however carefully we put it, that we appear to re-endorse that wicked treaty and to justify the evil policies of France towards world reconciliation during the last ten years. God knows, the danger from Germany is bad enough, but the dangers from France during the last few years have been equally grave. Therefore, during the next six months, the key issue to world peace is not so much to expose the wickedness of this or that country, as to make one last desperate effort to get a disarmament treaty signed, based on the idea of collective security. If that could be done we could very quickly deal with the menace from Germany. But to approach that menace directly, with France in her present mood, is simply to fan the flames of an early war. (Unpublished letter, Allen Papers.)

On 13 July 1934 WINSTON CHURCHILL told the House of Commons:

I am very glad that the Disarmament Conference is passing out of life into history. It is the greatest mistake to mix up disarmament with peace. When you have peace you will have disarmament. . . .

I hope, indeed, that we have now also reached the end of the period of the Government pressing France—this peaceful France with no militarism—to weaken her armed forces. I rejoice that the French have not taken the advice which has been offered to them so freely from various quarters, and which the Leader of the Opposition [Mr Lansbury] no doubt would strongly endorse. (*Hansard*.)

JOHN WHEELER-BENNETT wrote in 1934:

. . . it is not inconceivable that, faced with the dread of encirclement and in the grip of a serious economic crisis, the same leaders of Germany who shot down the 'conspirators' of 30 June without trial might, in a last desperate attempt to rally the country to them, indulge in some international excess, and thus, Samson-like, precipitate disaster. . . .

All hope of disarmament, or even of security, is vain until the gangster element has been eliminated from international politics. For if war was possible before, it has become one hundred per cent more so since the introduction of this new development. (*The Disarmament Deadlock*, p. 249.)

On 28 November 1934 WINSTON CHURCHILL declared in the House of Commons:

To urge preparation of defence is not to assert the imminence of war. On the contrary, if war were imminent preparations for defence would be too late. . . . What is the new great fact which has broken in upon us during the last 18 months? Germany is rearming. . . .

That mighty power is now equipping itself once again, 70,000,000 of people, with the technical apparatus of modern war. . . .

Let the Government give the lead, and the nation will not fail in the hour of need. (*Hansard*.)

In February 1935 a Government White Paper was prepared—announcing an accelerated rearmament programme. The Cabinet considered it, and modified its tone. On 26 February an official (perhaps it was SIR ROBERT VANSITTART) wrote to Baldwin:

. . . it seems to me that the one thing of supreme importance is that our public should be warned in no uncertain language.

I do therefore trust that the Cabinet may reconsider its attitude towards the purpose and form of the document, and address its mind not to gilding the pill for German consumption, but to ensuring that the pill provides the effective stimulation so much required by our sluggish-minded people. (*Stanley Baldwin* by G. M. Young, p. 194.)

On 4 March the White Paper was laid before Parliament. The Cabinet cautions had been accepted. For Churchill it was not enough. But for the Labour Party even the modified scale of rearmament was too much. On 11 March 1935 CLEMENT ATTLEE moved a resolution:

. . . that, in the opinion of this House, the policy of His Majesty's Government with respect to defence is completely at variance with the spirit in which the League of Nations was created to establish a collective world peace, gravely jeopardizes the prospect of any Disarmament Convention, and, so far from ensuring national safety, will lead to international competition and the insecurity thereby engendered and will ultimately lead to war. (*Hansard.*)

In the course of his speech ATTLEE said:

We believe in a League system in which the whole world should be ranged against an aggressor. If it is shown that someone is proposing to break the peace, let us bring the whole world opinion against her. . . . We do not think that you can deal with national armaments by piling up national armaments in other countries. (*Hansard.*)

SIR AUSTEN CHAMBERLAIN was blunt:

If war breaks out, if we become involved in a struggle, and if the Honourable Member for Limehouse [Mr Attlee] and his friends be sitting on the government bench while London is bombed, do you think he will hold the language he held today? . . . If he does, he will be one of the first victims of the war, for he will be strung up by an angry, and justifiably angry, populace to the nearest lamp-post. (*Hansard.*)

On 3 April the DAILY EXPRESS informed its readers:

The reaction of the British public to the Nazi rearmament will be plain and positive. They will demand that the British defences shall be built up by land, sea and air. They also mean to call to account the man responsible for the country's present weakness.

Mr MacDonald is Prime Minister and bears prime responsibility....
He let the Nazis build an air force, raise an army, lay down the keels of a navy. He has exposed Britain to Hitler's threats.

Can the people trust him to restore to them the power of defence? (*Daily Express.*)

WINSTON CHURCHILL spoke in the House of Commons on 22 May:

I have been told that the reason for the Government not having acted before was that public opinion was not ripe for rearmament. I hope that we shall never accept such a reason as that. The Government have been in control of overwhelming majorities in both Houses of Parliament. There is no vote they could not have proposed for the national defence which would not have been accepted with overwhelming strength. (*Hansard.*)

In 1935 Lord Londonderry was replaced as Secretary of State for Air by Lord Swinton. Some years later LORD LONDONDERRY wrote to Stanley Baldwin:

I think, looking back, that you, Neville and Ramsay lost confidence in me because you were frightened by the propaganda of Winston and Rothermere which asserted that the Germans were overwhelmingly strong. You had refused to listen to our advice on rearmament and I am sure you became anxious lest the propaganda might be correct, and that then you would be confronted with the charge of having failed in your duty of establishing the security of this country. I think that is why you threw me to the wolves. (Quoted in *Stanley Baldwin*, by G. M. Young, pp. 183–4.)

J. L. GARVIN, writing in *The Observer* on 2 June 1935, informed readers of:

... the plain undoubted probability that Europe within the next two or three years will be brought to the brink of war....

To restore national and Imperial Defence to something like the old basis of independent safety is by itself an undertaking of heroic size. It involves a large reconstruction of the Navy as well as the achievement of real Air parity....

No member of the present Administration is fit to be General Goering's opposite number. (*The Observer.*)

In 1935 the question arose (see p. 31) of imposing sanctions on Italy for her invasion of Abyssinia. Britain was in favour of sanctions. On 25 August WINSTON CHURCHILL wrote to Sir Samuel Hoare:

Where are the fleets? Are they in good order? Are they adequate? Are they capable of rapid and complete concentration? Are they safe? Have they been formally warned to take precautions? Remember you are putting extreme pressure upon a Dictator who may get into desperate straits. He may well measure your corn by his bushel. He may at any moment in the next fortnight credit you with designs far beyond what the Cabinet at present harbour. While you are talking judicious, nicely-graded formulas, he may act with violence. Far better put temptation out of his way. (*The Gathering Storm*, p. 133.)

On 9 February 1936 NEVILLE CHAMBERLAIN wrote:

If we were now to follow Winston's advice and sacrifice our commerce to the manufacture of arms, we should inflict a certain injury on our trade from which it would take generations to recover, we should destroy the confidence which now happily exists, and we should cripple the revenue. (*Life of Neville Chamberlain*, by Keith Feiling, p. 314.)

On 19 November 1935 SIR ROBERT VANSITTART wrote:

. . . *there is not a week to lose in our measures.* . . . The Germans are themselves giving us far clearer warning than we had before 1914; and we have the remedy—rearmament—in our hands if we are quick enough. (Colvin, *Vansittart*.)

On 17 May 1936 VANSITTART reiterated:

. . . our rearmament is not proceeding fast enough or notoriously enough; and considerable doubt is being cast upon it abroad. . . . (Colvin, *Vansittart*.)

On 5 November 1936 WINSTON CHURCHILL spoke in the House of Commons:

. . . when we speak of the reign of law we must mean a reign of law supported by adequate and, if possible by overwhelming force. The days of saving money on armaments have gone by. They may well return in happier conditions, but in this grim year 1936, and still more in its ominous successor, our aim, our task, is not to reduce armaments. It is something even more intense, even more vital, namely, to prevent war, if war can be staved off. (*Hansard*.)

Churchill's desire to rearm more swiftly was interpreted as a plea to join forces with other European Powers. NEVILLE CHAMBERLAIN answered him:

The present Government in particular have made it clear over and over again that we set our faces against the division of Europe into opposing blocs of Powers knit together in alliances, endeavouring ourselves to hold the balance of power between them or to ally ourselves with one or other of these blocs. We believe that the system has gone and is not likely to be revived. (*Hansard.*)

The Government would not take measures to rearm rapidly, or to seek allies. It refused to believe that war was imminent, or that, in time of crisis, war could not be averted by diplomacy. In justifying its inaction, it cited the so-called pacifist tone of the nation. Despite its vast majority, it did not wish to arouse the public to the need for armaments or alliances.

When Neville Chamberlain became Prime Minister in 1937 the pacifist view was firmly entrenched.

WILLIAM ASTOR told the House of Commons:

There is a large number of people who do not want to get mixed up in what may be a quarrel in Eastern Europe. It is conceivable that one might at the beginning of a war raise enthusiasm for fighting in a quarrel which was not our own, but it would be hard to keep the nation united in a modern war, when the soldiers knew that their wives and children were suffering, were being bombed and perhaps gassed . . . it is that deep strain of pacifism, the desire to keep out of quarrels, that animates the common people of the country which is one of the limiting facts in this question of expanding our commitments. (*Hansard.*)

On 23 May 1937 GENERAL IRONSIDE wrote in his diary:

The Recruiting campaign for the Regular Army is not going well. . . . What we want is a very definite statement from the Prime Minister that we need an Army. Then we can lay down what we want the Army for and how it is to be used. Then and only then shall we begin to get men of any sort. (*The Ironside Diaries*, p. 23.)

GENERAL IRONSIDE was invited to attend German Army manoeuvres in August 1937. His comments were encouraging:

I am quite sure that they are nowhere near ready for war, even at the tempo they have been going. If I were to hazard a guess, I might say 1940. . . .

There is no doubt that these people are not ready. Not for a big foe. I am sure of that. But will they try it out on the dog first? . . . the little nation that has been raped will scream in vain. I hope *we* shall then be strong enough to look after ourselves. We want a great fright to make us realise that we are in danger and then a knock or two to unite us all firmly. (*The Ironside Diaries*, pp. 26–28.)

On 15 November 1937 SIR ROBERT VANSITTART wrote:

There is not a man among us who does not feel that foreign policy cannot with any safety at all be continued on our present basis of material strength . . . I feel that you ought to point out to the Cabinet that it is steadily becoming more perilous to disregard the wisdom of Lord Grey. (Unpublished letter to Anthony Eden in author's possession.)

When Foreign Secretary in 1912 LORD GREY had written:

If you let your margin of strength fall below that which may be brought to bear on you rapidly, you are setting foreign policy a task which you ought not to set it. The risk of an attack on the United Kingdom stronger in force than we could meet with the ships we keep in Home waters is not one to be settled by diplomacy. (*Ibid*).

In 1912 Winston Churchill, as First Lord of the Admiralty, was raising the margin of Naval power to its needed level.[1] In 1937 the Service Ministers were less successful. Lord Swinton, the Air Minister, did his best, but the Treasury was against expense on rearmament.

The crisis year—1938—bore out the truth of Lord Grey's dictum. It might well have been Chamberlain's policy to warn Hitler against aggression in Europe. But Chamberlain knew that behind any strong words that he might utter lay a paucity of guns, a shortage of aeroplanes and nearly two decades of neglect and inefficiency. His diplomacy could not therefore be diplomacy through strength; and it was inevitable that Hitler's demands, however much even Chamberlain might want to resist them, would have to be met. Hitler's successes in 1938 were due in no small measure to the failure of Britain to rearm from 1933.

[1] Churchill tells the story of this in *The World Crisis* (vol. 1). His chief opponent was Lloyd George.

On 5 February 1938 GENERAL IRONSIDE wrote in his diary:

I don't wonder that our Government is in a fluster over its military affairs after their years of neglect in the face of so much warning. . . . (*The Ironside Diaries*, p. 47.)

On 13 March 1938 Hitler announced the dissolution of the Austrian Republic, and Austria's annexation to Germany. GENERAL IRONSIDE wrote in his diary:

The moral for us is that force is the only thing which tells with these two gangsters [Hitler and Mussolini]. If we are not ready to meet this force, then we shall go under. We have had ample warning. . . .

One hopes that the Government will not now wait for 'democratic mandates' and that they will leave no stone unturned to prepare the country. (*The Ironside Diaries*, p. 49.)

On 25 May 1938 WINSTON CHURCHILL told the House of Commons:

We are now in the third year of openly avowed rearmament. Why is it, if all is going well, there are so many deficiencies? Why, for instance, are the Guards drilling with flags instead of machine guns and anti-tank rifles? (*Hansard*.)

JOSIAH WEDGWOOD added:

Neglect of the air, neglect of alliances for defence, are evidences . . . that this Government, by complacence, have forgotten their responsibilities to their country and deserve the fate which must ultimately befall those who betray their country. (*Hansard*.)

SIR THOMAS MOORE replied:

. . . I think we must be thankful—I certainly am—that the Right Hon. Gentleman [Winston Churchill] is not today, in charge of a spending department which would give him the right and the facilities to indulge in some of the courses which he outlined. Otherwise, I fear that our Income Tax would not be 5s. in the £, but more than double that. . . .

I deprecate the practice of looking round for enemies and naming them. We have, I hope, no enemies in the world today . . . it is much better, if we fear a possible danger in Germany, for us to get on the same side of a friendly fence rather than to spit at each other across it. (*Hansard*.)

Despite the commonsense of General Ironside's demands for preparation, and despite Churchill's urgent pleas, neither the soldiers nor the politicians acted as if the hour were urgent. While Hitler's army appeared ready to attack Czechoslovakia, and as German anti-Czech propaganda grew louder throughout July and August, England still slept.

GENERAL IRONSIDE wrote in his diary on August 29:

In my talks with Gort [the Chief of the Imperial General Staff] I could see that he hasn't a proper grip of the situation. He has taken no steps for having a war H.Q. for the Army. None whatever. When I told him that I proposed to clear the White City he seemed surprised that I had done anything. . . . When I told him that it was the P.M.'s definite policy never again to send an Army to France he seemed surprised. He seemed out of his depth completely. (*The Ironside Diaries*, pp. 59–60.)

In September Britain took the initiative in persuading the Czechs to make wide concessions to Hitler—even if it meant handing over to Germany the German-speaking areas of Czechoslovakia which contained the Czech mountain defences, the Skoda armaments factory and the only geographic barrier between Czechoslovakia and Germany. The Czechs finally accepted British pressure, and surrendered the disputed territory.

The knowledge that Britain was too weak to fight alone (though, together with Czechoslovakia, France and perhaps Russia she might have fought) did not excuse, though it might explain, British policy.

GENERAL IRONSIDE wrote in his diary:

. . . it would be madness for us to expose ourselves to annihilation for the sake of the Czechs. (16 September.)

. . . the Czechs are to be sacrificed. I suppose one cannot blame the two Great Powers [Britain and France] for doing this. They made this ramshackle country and presumably they can unmake it. . . . (19 September.)

. . . To dismember Czechoslovakia . . . can only be called Peace Without Honour. (20 September.)

. . . our defences are so bad that we should go to any lengths to put off the struggle; so long, always, that we start in at once. (24 September.)

The Czechs, having learned that Britain and France would not support them if they resisted Germany, accepted the decision of the Four Powers at Munich (Britain, Germany, France and Italy), and handed over their German-speaking borderlands to the Nazis.

Neville Chamberlain hoped that, with the Czech crisis over, Anglo–German relations would improve. But he also realised that rearmament would have to be taken seriously.

NEVILLE CHAMBERLAIN told the House of Commons, at the conclusion of the 'Munich' debate, on 6 October 1938:

I do indeed believe that we may yet secure peace for our time, but I never meant to suggest that we should do that by disarmament. . . . Our past experience has shown us only too clearly that weakness in armed strength means weakness in diplomacy, and if we want to secure a lasting peace, I realise that diplomacy cannot be effective unless the consciousness exists, not here alone, that behind the diplomacy is the strength to give effect to it. (*Hansard*.)

On 24 October 1938 LORD HALIFAX told an audience at Edinburgh:

. . . if we are to succeed in bringing the world into smoother waters, we must face frankly the three possibilities that the future seems to hold. The first is war. The second is an armed peace. The third is a peace of understanding. We wish to escape the first, and we wish to achieve the third; but it may be that, just as Dante made the entry into Paradise through the way of Purgatory, so we, if we are to reach the true peace, have to pass through the stage of armed peace to get there. For let us remember peace will not come, like Christmas, just by waiting for it. (*Speeches on Foreign Policy by Viscount Halifax*, ed. by H. H. E. Craster, pp. 201–8.)

On 9 March 1939 SIR NEVILE HENDERSON wrote from Berlin:

So long as we go quietly on with our own defence preparations all will, in my opinion, be well. I believe the Germans want peace very badly, but it is just as well to remove temptation.

I wish we could rearm a little more quietly, but I suppose democracy is a bar to that. People in England are too much under the impression that Germany wants war. . . . (*British Documents* 3, VII, Appendix IV, no. IX. Letter to the Foreign Office.)

Conservative critics of rearmament accepted the need to rearm once it became Government policy. Labour M.P.s (with a few exceptions) did not. On the day German troops entered Prague CLEMENT ATTLEE told the House of Commons (14 March 1939):

However hard the Right Hon. Gentleman [the Air Minister] works, he cannot give us any security. We are building up insecurity. . . . We ought to face the fact that we cannot get security without total disarmament in the air. (*Hansard*.)

But the lessons of Prague could not be ignored—even by the staunchest believers in German goodwill. SIR NEVILE HENDERSON wrote on 17 June 1939:

So long as we go ahead steadily with our own military preparations, I do not think that we need particularly fear lest we encourage Ribbentrop and Company to think that we are weakening. In my opinion, Hitler is a man who draws his conclusions from and makes his decisions on actual facts rather than words. All the lung power in the world . . . counts for nothing with him compared with armed power. (*British Documents* 3, VI, Appendix I (iv), p. 706. Letter to Lord Halifax.)

Nazism

Governments must often negotiate and live on peaceful terms with other Governments whose domestic policies they find distasteful.

After 1918 Germany's Government was sufficiently parliamentary to meet with British approval. Despite internal troubles in Germany—inflation, revolution and a growing demand for the revision of Versailles—only the traditional anti-Germans in Britain hindered Anglo-German friendship. With the advent of Nazism in 1933 this easy friendship ended. The persecution inaugurated by the Nazis was offensive to most Englishmen. There were, however, strong groups who refused to admit any basic incompatibility between the British and German systems—who refused, above all, to believe that the differences were such that they would end inevitably in war. It was the hope of many sincere men that a *modus vivendi* would be possible.

In this section I look at the problems of the nature of Nazism, as it was known in Britain, and the reactions to Nazism, both at its violent outset in 1933 and during the years when Hitler was consolidating his power in Germany, not by violence alone, but by constructive programmes that met widespread approval outside Germany.

In 1939 Britain went to war, not to destroy Nazism, but to prevent the further spread of German domination in Europe. Many people wanted to see Nazi methods brought to a rapid end—but Germany's internal affairs were considered her own. Not the Jewish persecutions, but a rashly aggressive foreign policy, led to war in 1939. The Bishop of Durham saw the incompatibility of Nazism and the British way of life, but the idea of a war initiated by Britain to change the internal government of Germany was unthinkable.

For the traditional anti-Germans in Britain, Nazism was merely the proof of something they had known for a long time—that the Germans were unpleasant and untrustworthy. But for those who sought peace and co-operation with Germany—an entirely laudable aim after the holocaust of the Great War—Nazism posed a difficult problem. Should Britain cease to help Germany, cease to welcome her into the European community, cease to treat her as a worthy partner and trusted equal, because of her seemingly barbaric internal régime? The outbreak of violence in 1933 did not destroy the hope of Anglo-German friendship, though it weakened it. Each year saw more terror in Germany and fewer Englishmen willing to champion or to defend her. But even in 1939 some people held out hope of conciliation. By itself Nazism, practised inside the German borders, could not lead to war; but it weakened, to the point of destruction, British confidence in German sanity and British hope for Anglo-German friendships.

Anti-German passion ran high in England as the Great War ended. 'Hang the Kaiser' was a familiar cry. But perhaps the Kaiser was not enough. AUSTEN CHAMBERLAIN told a Birmingham audience on 29 November 1918:

I say until we are satisfied—and we cannot be satisfied until we have proved it—that in the German there is a changed heart and a changed mind, no single scapegoat can bear their sins. They have made their bed and they must lie upon it. (*The Life and Letters of Austen Chamberlain*, p. 129.)

There was a traditional anti-Germanism in Britain which had found an energetic exponent, before 1914, in Eyre Crowe, a Foreign Office official. The Great War confirmed EYRE CROWE in his beliefs: on 28 June 1920 he wrote:

It is dangerous, because futile, to enter into any discussion with Germans on whether the German Government 'wanted the war'. These words lend themselves to endless quibbles. No doubt Germany would have preferred to have what she aimed at, without a war. She found her aim could not be realized without war and therefore—no doubt, against her wishes—saw that war was the only method by which she could get what she wanted. A public discussion on this topic could only serve to increase existing prepossessions.

Moreover, German controversialists are not clean-handed. Our side in a discussion would act honestly and fairly. Experience of German methods does not allow us to believe that theirs would remain within such bounds. (*British Documents*, I, IX, no. 535, Note 7.)

Among those who claimed to follow in the 'Crowe tradition' was another diplomat, ROBERT VANSITTART, who was often in Germany in the 'twenties, and later recalled his impressions of post-Versailles conditions:

Germans, no longer able to beat up aliens, rounded on each other. . . . All Germany was demoralised. The churches had either lost their grip or misapplied it. Souls slipped through their fingers and found no calories in negation. The Universities bristled with the past. Sodomy, fostered by the pre-war army, was not only tolerated but flaunted on a scale hitherto unprecedented. As of old the capital was the chief plague-spot. . . .

One other unpleasantness, long suspected, became clear: Germany is more hard-working than Britain. Our people lacked the dynamism of jealousy. (*The Mist Procession*, p. 279.)

Others thought differently. EVELYN WRENCH had known Germany before the Great War, and visited it again in 1927:

From the moment I crossed the frontier on a Sunday morning I was in a new and unfamilar Germany, and a Germany which in many ways made a greater appeal to me. There was none of the overweening spirit of the pre-war decade. The German people had been through a gruelling experience. They no longer worshipped the false idol of national aggrandizement. The bullying and swaggering was gone. It seemed as if the war had not been in vain. On the horizon appeared the prospect of creating a new and better Europe with the help of Germany. (*I Loved Germany*, p. 50.)

LORD D'ABERNON, who had been British Ambassador in Berlin from 1920 to 1926 wrote, in 1929:

Can Germany be trusted? . . . much depends on the treatment accorded to Germany by foreign nations . . . today . . . it may safely be asserted that a considerable majority of the German people is resolutely in favour of peace. . . . The peace spirit in Germany required nourishment. (*An Ambassador of Peace*, vol. 1, p. 17.)

The optimism of 1929 was quickly lost. Nourishment was not at hand. Economic depression brought unemployment and bitterness. The social tension was quickly exploited by political extremists—among them the National Socialists—or Nazis. SIR HORACE RUMBOLD, British Ambassador in Berlin, commented on the Nazis early in 1932:

I was present when he [Bruning] made his speech [in the Reichstag] and was much struck by the unmannerly behaviour of the Nazis. They are like a lot of ill-bred schoolboys, who, to our ideas, behave like cads. The thought that the destinies of the country might be entrusted to such people is rather depressing, but we are far from that yet. (Private letter 27 February 1932.)

Unfortunately, the Nazis were soon to be in power. In March 1933 Adolf Hitler became German Chancellor, and quickly imposed his methods on a bewildered Germany.

On 2 May, 1933 the German trade unions were made illegal. Many communists and trade unionists were arrested and imprisoned without trial. Anti-semitism spread rapidly, with official support. On 1 April there was a one-day boycott against Jewish shops and professions. Jews were beaten up in the streets.

LADY VIOLET BONHAM-CARTER wrote:

The German atrocities make me feel quite ill with rage and shame. They also make me feel foolish at having been so steadfast a Pro-German ever since they became under-dogs. (Unpublished letter to Gilbert Murray, 4 April 1933, Murray Papers.)

EVELYN WRENCH had returned to Germany, and was in Berlin on 1 April 1933:

My first day in Berlin was one of the saddest in my life, it was the occasion of the first Government-organised boycott of the Jews. I could not believe my eyes. I had come across anti-semitism in Europe before, but I thought racial persecution belonged to another age. Half-civilised people might indulge in it but surely not the Germany that I had known. . . . After a few days I regained confidence in Germany's good intentions. Perhaps it would be more accurate to say that wishful thinking enabled me to accept the explanations given by supporters of the Nazi régime. I did not abate my intense dislike of many aspects of Nazi policy one iota, but I set it aside in my endeavour to see things from the German point of view. (*I Loved Germany*, p. 286.)

The British Press gave full publicity to the extraordinary developments in Germany. On 8 April 1933 the following report appeared in the MANCHESTER GUARDIAN:

The Terror seems to have been worst of all—worse even than in Berlin —in Cassel, in Silesia (where Heines, who was imprisoned on a charge of manslaughter and released by an amnesty, is in charge of the Brown Shirts), in Worms, and in many villages. A precise account of what has happened in the villages of Oberhessen alone during the last four weeks would make a terrible story. But it is impossible to establish more than a few cases, enquiry being made difficult by the general fear not only of reprisals but also of imprisonment. A few days ago a man was sentenced to a year's imprisonment for spreading the 'false rumour' that a Jew had been hanged by Brown Shirts—the 'rumour', as a matter of fact, was true: the Jew, a certain Mr ——, was beaten by Brown Shirts and hanged by his feet, so that his head was suspended off the ground. When the Brown Shirts had finished with him he was dead.

Any German who dare say a true word about the Terror in his own country runs the risk of a fearful beating, or long imprisonment or even death, and no one can reasonably be expected to run such a risk. But, as one of the victims of the Terror said to your correspondent to-day, it is impossible to remain silent even under threats. There is no reason why opinion in England and the United States should be hood-winked, and it is necessary to point out that letters or statements by German Jewish or Republican organisations or Societies saying that the Terror has been exaggerated are products of fear and intimidation and are therefore altogether unworthy of credence.

Thousands upon thousands of Germans have only one wish—to get out of the country. But the frontiers are being closed by the new pass-port regulations and escape is impossible except at great risk. Thus all Germany is being converted into a huge prison. (*Manchester Guardian*.)

SIR HORACE RUMBOLD was equally clear in his own mind about the implications of the new and accentuated violence:

Everything shows that this Nazi revolution has brought out some of the worst characteristics in the German character, namely, a mean spirit of revenge, brutality amounting in many cases to bestiality, and complete ruthlessness. The atmosphere here is thoroughly unpleasant . . . nobody feels himself safe or able to talk or write freely. One might almost be in Russia, but although the Bolshevists have tried to harry their political opponents almost to extinction, I do not remember that either they or Mussolini formed concentration camps into which to put pacifists and so-called Marxists.

It would be a mistake, however, to suppose that the Germans as a whole are in favour of Nazi activities in the direction of Jew-baiting etc. Many Germans are very unhappy and feel the stigma on their country. But they are impotent, and nothing was more remarkable than the complete collapse of all opposition to Hitler . . . An intelligent Jew expressed the opinion a few days after that, if there were elections in Germany today, Hitler would still further increase his following, in spite of recent events. (Unpublished letter to a diplomatic colleague, 11 April 1933, Rumbold Papers.)

In the House of Commons on 13 April 1933, M.P.s discussed Nazism for the first time. For two M.P.s at least Nazi brutality had international implications:

CLEMENT ATTLEE:

The suspicion among the smaller nations is that when four, five, or six great powers get together to try to settle their difficulties, those difficulties will be settled at the expense of the small nations. . . . I think this House and this country ought to say that we will not countenance for a moment the yielding to Hitler, and force, what was denied to Stresemann and reason. . . . The revision of the territorial settlement in favour of Germany would be an ironical pendant to the rape of China by Japan . . . when we come to this matter of Treaty revision, I hope that our Government will tell Germany straight out that if she wants any revision she must come with clean hands. (*Hansard.*)

SIR AUSTEN CHAMBERLAIN:

What is this new spirit of German nationalism? The worst of the all-Prussian Imperialism, with an added savagery, a racial pride, an exclusiveness which cannot allow to any fellow-subject not of 'pure Nordic birth' equality of rights and citizenship within the nation to which he belongs. Are you going to discuss revision with a Government like that? . . . Germany is afflicted by this narrow, exclusive, aggressive spirit, by which it is a crime to be in favour of peace and a crime to be a Jew. This is not a Germany to which we can afford to make concessions. (*Hansard.*)

SIR HORACE RUMBOLD was tireless in his efforts to explain the nature of Nazism to the Foreign Office and, through them, to the British Government:

The departure from Germany of so many writers, artists, musicians, and political leaders has created for the moment a kind of vacuum, for whatever may have been the shortcomings of the Democratic parties, they numbered among their following the intellectual life of the capital and nearly all that was original and stimulating in the world of art and letters.

One of the most inhuman features of the present campaign is the incarceration without trial of thousands of individuals whose political antecedents have rendered them obnoxious in the eyes of the new régime. The establishment of concentration camps . . . on a wholesale scale is a new departure in civilized countries. (*British Documents*, 2, v, no. 30, 13 April 1933.)

On 6 May 1933 SIR ROBERT VANSITTART commented on one of Rumbold's despatches:

The present régime in Germany will, on past and present form, loose off another European war just so soon as it feels strong enough. Their only fear is that they may be attacked before they are ready. Meanwhile it will endeavour to cog and lull so as better to eat the artichoke leaf by leaf. This is crude: but we are considering very crude people, who have few ideas in their noddles but brute force, militarism—and hot air to these ends . . . the end being war, for Hitler's fighting man. (Unpublished comment on a despatch of Sir Horace Rumbold's.)

Hitler's persecution of Communists and Social Democrats prompted VICTOR GOLLANCZ, a left-wing publisher, to give the maximum publicity to Nazi activity. In 1933 he published *The Brown Book of the Hitler Terror*, which gave details of Nazi behaviour as found in speeches, broadcasts, legal proceedings and the German Press.

Gollancz quoted from a popular Nazi song:

When Jewish blood spurts from under the knife,
Things will be twice as good as before.

The book gave many examples from the German Press of developments in Germany during 1933:

At the Tübingen council meeting on May 15th it was moved by a National Socialist that 'Jews and persons of foreign race be excluded from the use of the free municipal baths'. The motion was adopted with only three voting against it.

Berlin, March 8th. Yesterday evening sixty Nazi storm troopers occupied the stage of the Municipal Opera House, during the performance of *Rigoletto*, led by the famous conductor Busch. According to the account given by the *Vossische Zeitung*, the leader of the Nazis told the audience that in future he himself would direct the theatre, and that the conductor Strieger would conduct the orchestra instead of Busch. As Busch nevertheless attempted to continue conducting, a terrific uproar arose among the Nazis who were present, and Busch was compelled to leave. (*The Brown Book of the Hitler Terror*.)

SIR NORMAN ANGELL, author of *The Great Illusion* (1910) was profoundly disturbed by Nazism. In 1933 he reprinted his pre-war book with certain additions:

Throughout, Hitler has offered far more hates than cures, and nearly all observers agree that he did not need to offer cures if his hates were violent enough, and loud enough. (*The Great Illusion, 1933*, p. 11.)

Hitler has managed to persuade a great many Germans that his policy, with such items as the carefully planned ruin of those of his helpless fellow-countrymen who happen to belong to the race of Jesus Christ, represent the truest patriotism . . . (p. 54.)

Hitlerism, concluded Norman Angell, was an example of 'semi-mystic nationalism'.

People were not content to report what they saw, they sought also to explain it. EDGAR MOWRER published his explanation in 1933:

To the outside world Germany seems the country of organised science. But equally it is the country of rampant superstition. This people is rich in intellect, poor in common sense. It radiates intelligence, yet its several minds are open to the cosmic night. Through the openings drift in thousands of useful inventions and great ideas, fairy tales, philosophies, and perhaps even more fads and follies, distorted bat-like fancies, illusions, madnesses. It is essentially chaotic, illogical and romantic . . . in thought as in politics, this people is formless and therefore craves a form so strong that it cannot be broken. (*Germany Puts the Clock Back*, pp. 26, 27.)

SIR ARNOLD WILSON was invited to lecture in Germany in May 1934. On his return to England he broadcast his impressions on the B.B.C.:

I have seen German youth displaying in work and play an energy and an enthusiasm which, because it is wholly unselfish, is wholly good. Great dynamic forces have been developed, even greater forces are in reserve. Whatever be the aims of their leaders, I believe that the temper of the people is peaceful. They rejoice to feel and believe that they are again a united nation—able to look the world in the face. Our task is to do what we can individually to make it easier for them to shake hands with their neighbours. (*Walks and Talks Abroad*, p. 96.)

In 1934 WICKHAM STEED wrote *Hitler: Whence and Whither*. His conclusions were forthright:

German Nazism is the outcome of a morbid national mood. . . . It is a thoroughly unhealthy phenomenon. (p. 188.)
  The Nazi system in Germany . . . is a standing denial of what we mean by liberal civilisation. (p. 187.)

Steed discussed the history of anti-semitism in Germany (which he himself had first witnessed in 1892), and printed the Prussian Ministry of

Justice draft for the Nazi penal code. The draft had been published in Germany on 9 October 1933:

The first condition for the new legal order must be that henceforth no Jews, Negroes, or other coloured people can be absorbed into the German blood. The prohibition of blood-mingling must be so interpreted that mingling is forbidden with members of foreign blood-communities, or races whose isolation from German blood is to be regulated by law. (*Penal Code, draft*.)

WINSTON CHURCHILL feared that Nazi internal brutality would have international implications. On 13 July 1934 he told the House of Commons:

This is not the only Germany which we shall live to see, but we have to consider that at present two or three men, in what may well be a desperate position, have the whole of that mighty country in their grip, have that wonderful scientific, intelligent, docile, valiant people in their grip, a population of seventy millions; that there is no dynastic interest such as the monarchy brings as a restraint upon policy, because it looks long ahead and has much to lose; and that there is no public opinion except what is manufactured by those new and terrible engines —broadcasting and a controlled Press. Politics in Germany are not as they are over here. There you do not leave office to go into Opposition. You do not leave the Front Bench to sit below the Gangway. You may well leave your high office at a quarter of an hour's notice to drive to the police station, and you may be conducted thereafter very rapidly to an even graver ordeal. (*Hansard*.)

The sincerely held belief that Nazism would moderate was not born out by events, although it was not until 1945, when Allied troops saw the concentration camps for the first time, that the full extent of Nazi horror was realised. Suspicion of Nazism, however had remained constant in some minds ever since the revelations of 1933.

SIR CLIVE WIGRAM wrote to Sir Eric Phipps on 16 January 1935:

His Majesty [King George V] feels that we must not be blinded by the apparent sweet reasonableness of the Germans, but be wary and not taken unawares. (*King George V*, by Sir Harold Nicolson, p. 522.)

LORD LOTHIAN sought to explain rather than to condemn. On 1 February 1935 he wrote:

In some degree the brutality of National Socialism is the reaction to the treatment given to Germany herself since the war. I believe the best way of restoring reasonable rights to the Jews in Germany is not to counter hate by hate but to undermine the source of the evil aspects of National Socialism by giving to Germany her rightful place in Europe. I think this is the solution which the greatest of all the Jews would have prescribed, though it is one, I admit, that his followers and compatriots have seldom put into practice. (Unpublished letter in Lothian Papers.)

On 22 May 1935 LORD WINTERTON told the House of Commons:

The German nation, as a whole, possesses, in a mental and physical sense, a virility and determination which has seldom, if ever, been exceeded in the world's history. No one who has any friendship with individual Germans, as I have, can doubt that. See the German boys in school; see the German young men and women; see the magnificent physique and determination of these people . . . her grievances arising from the Versailles Treaty are, in her judgement, still unredressed. . . . Vocal and influential sections of opinion in this country, such as trade unions, Jewish organisations, and the Labour party have, whether rightly or wrongly, condemned the leader of Germany in violent language. Let us remember in this connection that Germany is sensitive to criticism. (*Hansard.*)

On 1 July 1935 the MANCHESTER GUARDIAN described the growing terror in Germany. This report—one of a number which they published in 1935—dealt with a Gestapo 'office' in Hamburg, and a political prisoner:

As the prisoner refused to give information he was tortured. His head was wrapped in a wet cloth that was knotted so tightly across his mouth that his teeth cut into his lips and his mouth bled profusely.

He was held by three assistants while the official and another assistant took turns in beating him with a flexible leather-covered steel rod ('Stahlrute'). When he fainted from pain and loss of blood he was brought to by means of various other tortures.

His mouth became so dry that tongue, lips, and gums seemed to stick together. A rag soaked in turpentine was pushed into his mouth. He was asked, 'Are you going to speak up?' He said nothing, whereupon he was again tortured. But he could not be induced to speak. He was told that he might write a letter to his wife, as he would never see her again. The assistants fingered their pistols and discussed which of them should shoot the prisoner. But he remained silent. He was released some time afterwards.

A fellow-prisoner, aged between 55 and 60, a man named Ott, from Altona, was tortured in the same way, and died under the treatment (perhaps from heart failure). (*Manchester Guardian*.)

ADMIRAL SIR BARRY DOMVILE wrote in 1935:

The Nazis have treated the Jews with great harshness and tactlessness, thereby alienating the sympathy of other countries, but I am very far from adopting the sloppy sentimental attitude towards the Jewish race which is so popular in this country. Because we ourselves are tolerant of the aliens and Jews in our midst to the point of stupidity, that is no reason for our being so intolerant with the policy of others. . . . Ask any little man you know of his experience in working with Jews—I have asked a good many, and they would all go a long way to deal with a Gentile in preference. Jewish ways are not our ways, neither are their thoughts our thoughts, and it is no good pretending they are. . . .

> Hey diddle diddle
> Europe's a riddle
> Musso cries out for the moon.
> The Aryans laugh to see their chance,
> But the Jews get away with the spoon!
>
> (and always will).
> (*By and Large*, pp. 246–9.)

Sir Eric Phipps followed Sir Horace Rumbold as Ambassador in Berlin, and was an equally outspoken opponent of Nazism.

On 24 May 1936 Stanley Baldwin asked his close friend Thomas Jones: 'What are we to do?' THOMAS JONES replied:

If it is our policy to get alongside Germany, then the sooner Phipps is transferred elsewhere the better. He should be replaced by a man . . . unhampered by professional diplomatic tradition, able of course to speak German, and to enter with sympathetic interest into Hitler's aspirations. (*A Diary with Letters*, p. 208.)

LORD LONDONDERRY resented the anti-Germanism of certain members of the Government. On 4 February 1937 he wrote:

I have been very careful in my relations with Germany never to adopt any attitude, which Anthony Eden unfortunately does, of hectoring and lecturing and criticising what they do. (Unpublished letter to Lord Allen of Hurtwood, Allen Papers.)

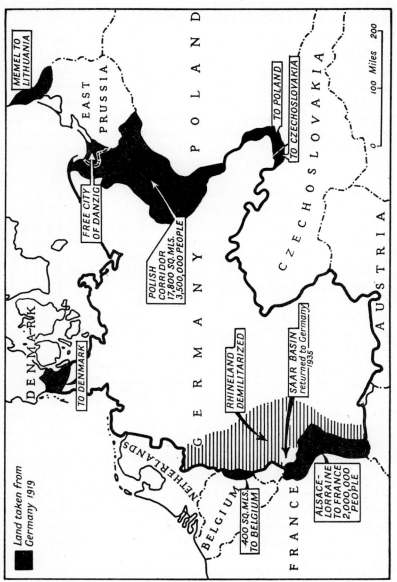

The German Problem 1935

Land taken from Germany 1919

MEMEL TO LITHUANIA

EAST PRUSSIA

POLAND

TO POLAND

TO CZECHOSLOVAKIA

CZECHOSLOVAKIA

FREE CITY OF DANZIG

POLISH CORRIDOR 17,800 SQ.MLS. 3,500,000 PEOPLE

DENMARK

TO DENMARK

GERMANY

RHINELAND DEMILITARIZED

SAAR BASIN returned to Germany 1935

AUSTRIA

NETHERLANDS

BELGIUM

400 SQ.MLS. TO BELGIUM

ALSACE-LORRAINE TO FRANCE 2,000,000 PEOPLE

FRANCE

100 Miles 200

BERTRAND RUSSELL adopted a pacifist standpoint, which he was later to abandon. On 3 March 1937 he wrote:

Having remained a pacifist while the Germans were invading France and Belgium in 1914, I do not see why I should cease to be one if they do it again. The result of our having adopted the policy of war at that time is not so delectable as to make me wish to see it adopted again. You feel 'they ought to be stopped'. I feel that, if we set to work to stop them, we shall, in the process, become exactly like them and the world will have gained nothing. Also, if we beat them, we shall produce in time some one as much worse than Hitler as he is worse than the Kaiser. (Unpublished letter to Gilbert Murray, Murray Papers.)

GEOFFREY DAWSON wrote, on 23 May 1937:

I should like to get going with the Germans.

I simply cannot understand why they should apparently be so much annoyed with *The Times* at this moment. I spend my nights in taking out anything which I think will hurt their susceptibilities and in dropping in little things which are intended to soothe them. (Unpublished letter to Lord Lothian, Lothian Papers.)

On 1 June 1937 NEVILE HENDERSON, who had become British Ambassador to Berlin in May, spoke, in Berlin, of British attitudes to Nazism:

...far too many people have an erroneous conception of what the National Socialist régime really stands for. Otherwise they would lay less stress on Nazi dictatorship and much more emphasis on the great social experiment which is being tried out.... (*The Times*, 2 June 1937.)

On 8 June ARTHUR HENDERSON, a Labour M.P., challenged Nevile Henderson in the House of Commons:

Is it an erroneous conception of what the National-Socialist party in Germany stands for to allege that they have oppressed the Jews, suppressed all political opposition, placed many of their opponents in concentration camps, and destroyed free trade-unionism? (*Hansard.*)

SIR HORACE RUMBOLD wrote to Geoffrey Dawson on 13 June 1936:

I have rather come to the conclusion that the average Englishman— whilst full of common-sense as regards internal affairs—is often muddle-headed, sloppy and gullible when he considers foreign affairs. One often hears such phrases as 'the Germans are so like us'. Nothing is more untrue. I could quote many points of difference. For one thing Germans have a streak of brutality which is quite absent in the ordinary Englishman. And Germans like to put up with things which are repugnant to the average man of this country. My point is, therefore, that we should know the people with whom we propose to deal.

Now Hitler has quite consistently applied the principles of *Mein Kampf* in Germany herself. He has now got to apply them in his foreign policy and that's where the trouble is coming. The value to us of an understanding with Germany is not only that it may bring peace and stability in Western Europe but that it may act as a drag on Hitler's adventures in Central and Eastern Europe. Once he embarks on any adventure in those regions war is, to my mind, a dead certainty. The ordinary Englishman does not realise that the German is an inexorable Oliver Twist. Give him something and it is a jumping-off ground for asking for something else. (*Geoffrey Dawson and Our Times* by Evelyn Wrench, p. 334.)

HERBERT HENSLEY HENSON, Bishop of Durham, doubted whether war could be avoided between totalitarianism and democracy. On 10 April 1938 he wrote to Lord Londonderry:

The suspicion grows on my mind that the well-meant and attractive policy of avoiding the division of Europe or rather of the civilized world into rival 'ideologies' must ultimately fail before the *inherent necessity of agreement in ultimate principle if harmony is to be preserved*. Abraham Lincoln's declaration about the American Union may be justly applied to modern civilization:

'A house divided against a house cannot stand. I believe this government cannot endure half slave and half free. I do not expect the house to fall but I expect it will cease to be divided. It will become all one thing or all the other.'

The *principle* of democracy is personal freedom; the *principle* of dictatorship (No. 1: Bolshevist, No. 2: Fascist) is personal servitude. One or other must be supreme; they cannot co-exist in amiable co-operation in a civilized world so closely linked as is the civilized world today. I wish a clearer expression could be given to the sense of *moral nausea* which is growing in many minds in England, as the abominable oppression of minorities, Jewish and Christian, proceeds and advances in Germany. This is one of the '*imponderables*' which Bismarck warned politicians not to neglect. *It will defeat the diplomats of compromise in the long run.* (*Ourselves and Germany*, by Lord Londonderry, p. 176.)

During the Czech crisis of September 1938 it seemed that Britain and Germany would be at war. War was avoided, but many thought it was inevitable. NEVILLE CHAMBERLAIN was optimistic however. On 13 December 1938 he told members of the Foreign Press Association at a dinner in London:

History teaches us that no form of Government ever remains the same. The change may come by slow degrees, or it may come suddenly, like an explosion. But change in one form or another is inevitable, and it would seem to follow, therefore, that we should be careful not to shut ourselves off from contact with any country on account of a system which, in the course of time, may well undergo such modifications as to render it very different from what it is today. (*Manchester Guardian*, 14 December 1938.)

War came, however, in September 1939, and did not end until the destruction of the Nazi system in 1945. Perhaps the shrewdest comment on Nazism was made by SIR NORMAN ANGELL, in a conversation with Harold Nicolson at the height of the Czech crisis:

In the *Great Illusion* I tried to teach people that war never paid. We shall go into this war knowing that it doesn't pay. But Nazi domination pays even less. (Harold Nicolson, diary entry, unpublished, for 26 September 1938.)

Italy

Early in 1925 AUSTEN CHAMBERLAIN wrote of Mussolini:

... if I ever had to choose in my own country between anarchy and dictatorship I expect I should be on the side of the dictator. In any case I thought Mussolini a strong man of singular charm and I suspected of not a little tenderness and loneliness of heart. ...

I believe him to be accused of crimes in which he had no share, and I suspect him to have connived unwillingly at other outrages which he would have prevented if he could. But I am confident that he is a patriot and a sincere man; I trust his word when given and I think we might easily go far before finding an Italian with whom it would be as easy for the British Government to work. (*Life of Sir Austen Chamberlain*, by Sir Charles Petrie, pp. 295–6.)

HUGH DALTON wrote in his memoirs, after recalling visits to Italy and Germany in 1933:

Italian Fascism, just because it was Italian, was much less intense, more casual, and therefore less evil, than German Nazism. Nor could Italy, standing alone, ever be the grim threat that Germany soon would be. And many Germans, but very few Italians, were really mad. (*The Fateful Years*, p. 41.)

SIR ROBERT VANSITTART first met Mussolini in 1934. He wrote of him:

He was a bounder. But bounding is no sin in the sun. He liked women and advancement; others have had the same tastes with less fulfilment. He enjoyed good looks with some good nature and an occasional sense of humour. ...

He was having too good a time to want trouble; and a *jouisseur's* repugnance to war is more reliable than a pacifist's because it is more practical. (*Mist Procession*.)

On 2 October 1935 Italy invaded Abyssinia. The British Cabinet were divided. Anthony Eden wanted to work with the League of Nations, and to impose strong sanctions upon Italy. SIR SAMUEL HOARE was not convinced that this was the right policy.

He told the House of Commons on 3 December 1935:

We have no wish to humiliate Italy or to weaken it. Indeed we are most anxious to see a strong Italy in the world, and Italy that is strong morally, physically and socially, and is able to contribute to the world valuable assistance. . . . We have not the least desire to interfere in the internal affairs of Italy, and we are most anxious to see a strong Italy governed by a strong government in whatever form the Italian people might desire. (*Hansard.*)

Four days later Hoare went to Paris, where he discussed, with Pierre Laval, a plan to end the war by a compromise which involved giving

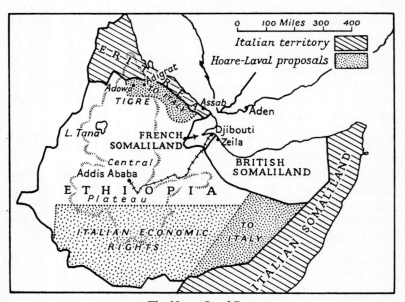

The Hoare–Laval Pact

Italy a large portion of Abyssinia. When the plan was known there was such an outcry in Britain that Hoare was forced to resign. It was perhaps the most decisive 'success' of public opinion in the inter-war years. Once Hoare had gone, opinion hardened against Italy.

SIR ERIC PHIPPS wrote from Berlin on 6 November 1935:

Hitherto it has always been assumed that Italy would form part—indeed an indispensable part—of any counterpoise to Germany. That position was reached at Stresa; but the assumption is no longer possible. No one can foretell what either her tendencies or capacity will be as a result of her war with Abyssinia and her quarrel with the League. All we can say is that their view certainly renders any prospect of an effective encirclement of Germany even more doubtful than before. (Unpublished letter. Copy in the author's possession.)

On 6 May 1936 WINSTON CHURCHILL told the House of Commons:

Abyssinia is now in the hands of Italy. Italy has by violence made herself responsible for the welfare of the Ethiopian people. In trying further to impoverish and weaken the Italian nation we may only weaken the resources out of which the Ethiopian can be nourished and sustained, and embitter and worsen their fate. (*Hansard.*)

All hope of Anglo-Italian co-operation was not lost; SIR ROBERT VANSITTART wrote, in a Foreign Office Memorandum, on 21 May 1936:

Italy may well in the future be dangerous, but she has not yet the same striking force or resolve or reserve of power as Germany. Mussolini has made his first advances to his fellow dictator across the Alps; but unless we drive him into an active and offensive co-operation with Hitler, we are entitled to hope that he will not be anxious to take the high road to Berlin. We shall have to compromise with Mussolini, for we can never compromise securely or even live safely with Dictator Major, if we are at loggerheads with Dictator Minor. (Colvin, *Vansittart.*)

On 25 July 1936 Mussolini agreed to send military aid to General Franco, one of the leaders of the Nationalist Rebellion in Spain. Britain was against any other powers intervening in the Spanish Civil War, and on 9 September 1936 convened a meeting of the Non-Intervention Committee in London. On 23 October 1936 Britain accused Italy of having landed aircraft on the Spanish island of Majorca. The protest was ineffectual, and after the arrival of Russian arms in October and November Mussolini decided, on 6 December 1936, to intensify Italian aid. There were some 14,000 Italian troops in Spain by the end of January 1937. Britain, unable to restrict Italian aid to the Nationalists, sought assurances that Italy had no intention to alter the balance of sovereignty in the Mediterranean. Britain sought to avoid a quarrel with Italy over Italy's patronage of General Franco—a patronage resented by many in Britain who sympathised with the Republican Government which Franco sought to overthrow.

The British Government's decision not to antagonise Anglo–Italian relations on account of Spain led to the Anglo–Italian Agreement—known as the GENTLEMAN'S AGREEMENT, of 2 January 1937:

His Majesty's Government in the United Kingdom and the Italian Government:

Animated by a desire to contribute increasingly, in the interests of the general cause of peace and security, to the betterment of relations between them. . . .

Disclaim any desire to modify or, so far as they are concerned, to see modified the *status quo* as regards national sovereignty of territories in the Mediterranean area;

Undertake to respect each other's rights and interests in the same area;

Agree to use their best endeavours to discourage any activities liable to impair the good relations which it is the object of the present declaration to consolidate.

This declaration is designed to further the end of peace and is not directed against any other power. (*Documents on International Affairs 1937*, ed. by Stephen Meald, p. 87.)

On 19 July 1937 ANTHONY EDEN made it clear in the House of Commons that Britain did not seek to challenge Italy in the Mediterranean:

While we are determined to defend our own interests we have no intention of challenging those of others. That is why we made with Italy the Mediterranean Agreement of last January. We stand by that agreement. If the Mediterranean is for us a main arterial road—and it is—yet there is plenty of room for all on such a road. If we intend to maintain our place on it—and we do—we have no intention of seeking to turn anybody else off it. Least of all do we wish to interfere with those who geographically dwell upon it. There is ample room for all. . . .

This country has no intention of pursuing towards any other country a policy either of aggression or of revenge. Such a possibility has never occurred to the British people. The word 'vendetta' has no English equivalent. (*Hansard.*)

Italy continued to give the Nationalists, who now controlled over half of Spain, as much military aid as they could. On 14 September 1937 Britain and France agreed at Nyon to patrol the Mediterranean west of

Malta, and to attack suspicious submarines that might be gun-running into Spain. On 27 September 1937 Italy was allotted a patrol zone by Britain and France, which enabled her to send supplies to Franco through Majorca without being watched. Thus only aid to the Republican Government (from Russia, or from private individuals in Europe) would be stopped. Britain agreed to make this important concession to Italy in return for a promise by Mussolini that he would withdraw his troops by stages from Spain. Neville Chamberlain accepted Mussolini's promise; Anthony Eden advised against doing so.

SIR SAMUEL HOARE described one cause of friction between Chamberlain and Eden—the visit of Chamberlain's sister-in-law, Lady Chamberlain, to Rome in the autumn of 1937:

Austen Chamberlain had formed a friendship with Mussolini whilst visiting Italy during a yachting holiday. Lady Chamberlain, therefore, was assured of a friendly welcome by the Duce . . . whether it was Mussolini's astuteness in playing upon her susceptibilities, or her own excessive zeal in pressing her brother-in-law's policy of better Anglo–Italian relations, the result was unfortunate. Mussolini assumed that we were ready for negotiations with little or no preliminary discussion, and that Chamberlain's move disclosed a policy of weakness. . . . (*Nine Troubled Years*, p. 259.)

Eden wished to negotiate with Mussolini, but only from a position of strength.

On 18 February 1938 Chamberlain told Eden that he wanted to open conversations with Italy, without first insisting, as Eden wished, on a withdrawal of Italian forces from Spain. ANTHONY EDEN recorded at the time:

N[eville] C[hamberlain] made it clear that he knew exactly what he wanted to do. He wanted to . . . open conversations at once. . . . I demurred, pointing out that we had still made very little progress in the Spanish affair. . . .

N.C. became very vehement, more vehement than I have ever seen him, and strode up and down the room saying with great emphasis, 'Anthony, you have missed chance after chance. You simply cannot go on like this.'

I said, 'Your methods are right if you have faith in the man you are negotiating with.' N.C. replied, 'I have.' (*Facing the Dictators*, p. 582.)

Eden resigned on 19 February 1938. In his memoirs he cites the opinion of the historian SIR LEWIS NAMIER as corroboration of his attitude:

The more *empressement* the British Government showed to gain Mussolini's friendship, the more he was convinced of their timorous weakness and the more he despised them. A firm attitude and a strictly correct approach, such as are of the tradition of British diplomacy might have disconcerted Mussolini: courting him swelled his self-important conceit. (Quoted in *Facing the Dictators*, p. 595.)

NEVILLE CHAMBERLAIN wrote to his sister:

I have gradually arrived at the conclusion that at bottom Anthony did not want to talk either with Hitler or Mussolini, and as I did, he was right to go. (Quoted in *Nine Troubled Years*, by Viscount Templewood, p. 279.)

On 8 April 1938 CHAMBERLAIN spoke at Birmingham:

During recent weeks we have been engaging in conversations . . . with the Italian Government, with the result that a whole cloud of suspicions and misunderstandings has been blown away. There is today a good prospect of restoring those old friendly relations which, until they were recently broken, has lasted so long that they had become almost traditional between our two countries. . . .

I only ask you to have a little patience, to wait a little longer . . . before our agreement with Italy is concluded and published, and then, if you are not of my opinion, if you do not believe that it is not the Prime Minister who has been fooled, but the Socialists and Liberals who have fooled themselves, I will be prepared to eat my hat. (*The Times*, 9 April 1938.)

The second Anglo–Italian Agreement was signed on 16 April 1938. Agreement was reached, in the phrase of the Protocol, 'on questions of mutual concern': these included the Anglo–Italian Agreement of 2 January 1937 [see p. 88] which was confirmed. It was decided to begin discussions as soon as possible on all matters concerning colonial trade; and for Britain to consider recognising Italian sovereignty over Abyssinia; it was agreed to have an annual exchange of military information 'regarding any major prospective administrative movements or redistribution of their respective naval, military and air forces'; and it was agreed that neither Italy nor Britain would use propaganda 'in order to injure the interests of the other'. (*Documents on International Affairs 1938*, ed. by Monica Curtis, vol. i, pp. 141–56.)

NEVILLE CHAMBERLAIN told the House of Commons on 2 May 1938:

The Agreement is a step towards general appeasement. . . . Today there is a new Italy, an Italy which, under the stimulus of the personality of Signor Mussolini, is showing a new vigour, in which there is apparent new vision and new efficiency. . . . I believe we may look forward to a friendship with the new Italy . . . as firmly based, as that by which we were bound to the old. (*Hansard*.)

During the Debate LEO AMERY said:

I believe that this Agreement ought to be welcomed by everyone in this country. It renews a friendship which goes back to the great days of Italy's effort to reassert herself as a nation. . . . There is no real essential ground of quarrel between this country and Italy, and there is every ground for our co-operation. (*Hansard*.)

SIR ARCHIBALD SINCLAIR added:

Now, apparently, we are going to object to the Emperor of Abyssinia being represented at the next meeting of the League on the ground— the infamously mean ground—that he is in arrears with his subscriptions. If a just balance-sheet was struck of the mutual obligations of the League and the Emperor, it would not be the Emperor who would be found to be in arrears. (*Hansard*.)

R. A. BUTLER put the Government case:

We are seeking to do away with disagreements and to clear the ground so that the plant of peace may have a chance to grow. No one wants war, but hate and derogatory remarks such as we have heard today will never succeed in banishing war between nations. Hate only leads to war and, if civilisation means anything, surely it leads us towards the goal of sympathy and restraint. (*Hansard*.)

On 18 May 1938 in the House of Lords LORD HALIFAX insisted that Anglo–Italian relations could still improve:

. . . it is not to say that I or we approve of Italian intervention in Spain, any more than we approve of Italian action in Ethiopia. We have always made it our purpose to get rid of all foreigners from Spain. . . .

but . . . we have never asked or expected that the Italians should withdraw unilaterally, on their own, and provided that we are satisfied, as we are, that the Italian Government do not mean to use Spain for the alteration of the Mediterranean *status quo* when the Spanish trouble is over, we do not see why the fact that the Italian Government takes a strong view on one side, as against a strong view taken by large sections of opinion in this country on the other side, should preclude us from an attempt to improve our relations with them over the wider international field. (*Hansard.*)

With the Czech crisis becoming acute during the summer of 1938, Anglo–German relations became paramount, and Italy's position as a potential friend was neglected. Italian hostility to a major European war was seen when Mussolini, at Britain's request, helped to sponsor the Munich conference—at which Britain, France, Italy and Germany decided where the German–Czech frontier should run. But this was really an Anglo–German decision. Italy, though anxious to be seen on the side of peace, was clearly only a minor power. As such, her friendship ceased to be rated as highly as it had been in 1937.

In April 1939, after Hitler had occupied Prague, Mussolini, as if to show that he, too, was capable of military success, invaded Albania.

On 13 April 1939 Members of Parliament debated the Albanian invasion.

NEVILLE CHAMBERLAIN was unwilling to declare the Anglo–Italian Agreement at an end, but said:

I frankly confess my deep disappointment at an action by the Italian Government which has cast a shadow over the genuineness of their intentions to carry out their undertakings. (*Hansard.*)

All was not necessarily gloom however.

WINSTON CHURCHILL said:

I am still not convinced that Italy has made up her mind . . . to be involved in a mortal struggle with Great Britain and France in the Mediterranean. (*Hansard.*)

CHAMBERLAIN wrote to Edouard Daladier on 13 July 1939:

I feel that Mussolini is the one man who can influence Hitler to keep the peace. (*British Documents* 3, VI, no. 371.)

This view was challenged in the Foreign Office.

SIR PERCY LORAINE, British Ambassador in Rome, thought the chances of Anglo–Italian co-operation were becoming increasingly remote. On 21 July 1939 he wrote to Lord Halifax:

. . . while we have remained relatively passive, the Italian Government have not. They have drawn yet closer to Germany . . . they resent our negotiations with Russia; their Press loads us with ridicule and calumny. . . . To all appearances, therefore, the Duce has gritted his teeth to see his German partner right through . . . and is behaving as if he no longer valued our friendship or feared our hostility. . . .

It would thus be possible to make out a pretty convincing case for taking up a more active and considerably less tolerant attitude towards Italy herself. . . . (*British Documents* 3, VI, no. 396.)

LORD HALIFAX replied by describing a suggestion that had been made to him by Colonel William Long that 'it would not be impossible to draw Mussolini out of the Axis'. He wrote to Sir Percy Loraine on 25 July 1939:

This, in his view could be done if (a) the French would meet them over Djibuti and the Suez Canal, (b) we would give Italy a guarantee for the Brenner and (c) we would give Italy a loan of unspecified amount.

The naked idea is no doubt one that has constantly passed through your mind as it has through mine. . . . I should rather like your mind about it, as also on the point of how, on the assumption we do not dismiss the idea off-hand as fantastic, it would be at all conceivable that any such approach, constituting as it would so cynical a comment on Italian morality, could possibly be made. (*British Documents* 3, VI, no. 447.)

But SIR PERCY LORAINE replied to Halifax's query on 1 August 1939:

I think the real answer is contained in your speech at Chatham House of June 29. . . .

'. . . Unless all countries do in fact desire a settlement, discussions would only do more harm than good. . . . The threat of military force is holding the world to ransom and our immediate task is . . . to resist aggression.'

I fear that Italy does not today fulfil the conditions you lay down. . . .

One must ask too what would be the effect on our friends who have joined or are expected to join the peace front. Might it not appear to them dangerous wobbling and be likened to the fatal tactics of buying off the barbarians employed by the ancient Roman Empire? . . .

Let us, now that we are strong . . . keep Mussolini uncomfortable . . . until the balance of armed strength has turned visibly against the Axis powers, it is best for you to maintain your *silence menaçant* in London, and me my *silence souriant* in Rome. (*British Documents* 3, VI, no. 501.)

Neville Chamberlain commented on this: 'a very sensible letter'.

Chamberlain, too, had no more illusions about asking Italy to play a positive pro-British role. Her neutrality was to be welcomed—her other activities deprecated.

On 31 August 1939 Mussolini suggested a conference, to be held on 5 September, to revise the Versailles Treaty. CHAMBERLAIN replied at once:

. . . that it was impossible to agree to a conference under the threat of mobilised armies . . . a preliminary condition in any case would have to be a measure of demobilisation. (*British Documents* 3, VII, no. 590.)

Thus Italy's last attempt to avert a European war was turned down.

When Germany invaded Poland, Italy stood aside. She did not declare war on England nor England on her. Only when the fall of France was imminent, in 1940, did Italy join openly with Germany.

Hitler

In 1924 Adolf Hitler completed his lengthy, repetitive book, *Mein Kampf* (My Struggle), in which he set out his political philosophy, his analysis of recent history and his autobiography. *Mein Kampf* was first published in England in 1933 and was widely read. Those who believed what Hitler said in it to be a true statement of his views naturally saw him as someone to be feared. Others argued that his book was the product of passion and bitterness (it was written while Hitler was in prison) and that once in power he would discard its extremist claims. But there is no evidence that Hitler ever moderated his views, except for the purpose of temporary political expediency. He certainly encouraged Germans to read his book throughout his twelve years as Chancellor (1933–45). It was a strange yet common example of the power of self-deception that Englishmen could ignore, or try to explain away, the views which Hitler had taken such pains to express. Hitler's advocacy of an Anglo–German alliance was perhaps an attractive counter to his crude racial doctrine.

Hitler welcomed English visitors, and made exceptionally successful use of their visits. He could appear so charming, so sensible, so calm, even so ordinary, that the visitor, who might be expecting screams and extremism, was often convinced of the Führer's peaceful intentions. The skill with which he lulled his frequent, and important, visitors into an acceptance of his wisdom and sanity shows how easily a statesman can disarm critics and wise men by a show of friendship. In *Mein Kampf* Hitler's views were clearly expressed.

The English edition was 80,000 words long, the German edition 230,000; but the basis of Hitler's philosophy was evident in both. In the shortened English edition of 1933, published by Hurst and Blackett, HITLER wrote:

If the Jew, with the help of his Marxian creed, conquers the nations of this world, his crown will be the funeral wreath of the human race. . . . Thus did I now [as a young man in Vienna] believe that I must act in the sense of the Almighty Creator: By fighting against the Jews I am doing the Lord's work. (*Mein Kampf*, pp. 35–6.)

[Democracy] can only be pleasing or profitable to mendacious crawlers who avoid the light of day, and it must be hateful to any good, straightforward man who is ready to take personal responsibility. . . . None but a Jew can value an institution which is as dirty and false as he is himself. (*Mein Kampf*, p. 47.)

If we divide the human race into three categories—founders, maintainers and destroyers of culture—the Aryan stock alone can be considered as representing the first category. . . . Blood-mixture, and the lowering of the racial level which accompanies it, are the one and only causes why old civilisations disappear. . . . The exact opposite of the Aryan is a Jew. (*Mein Kampf*, pp. 121–4.)

The Jew forcibly drives all competitors off the field. Helped by his innate greedy brutality, he sets the Trades Union movement on a footing of brute force. Anyone with intelligence enough to resist the Jewish lure is broken by intimidation, however determined and intelligent he might be. (*Mein Kampf*, pp. 128–9.)

. . . only two States are left as possible friends to us: Great Britain and Italy . . . it is these two States whose own most natural interests are least in opposition to the conditions essential to the existence of the German nation, and are, in fact, to a certain extent, identical with them. . . . Our Jewish press succeeded again and again in concentrating hatred on Great Britain, and many a silly German bullfinch flew only too readily on to the bird-lime made ready by the Jews. (*Mein Kampf*, pp. 247–8.)

. . . the Jew is today a rebel in England, and the struggle against the Jewish world menace will be started there also. (*Mein Kampf*, p. 252.)

We must not forget that Bolshevists are blood-stained. . . . The results of an alliance with England and Italy would be directly opposite to those of one with Russia. . . . The new Anglo–German–Italian Alliance would hold the reins, and France would cease to do so . . . the new Alliance would include States who possess technical qualities that mutually supplement each other . . . we shall and must succeed, if the knowledge of the necessity of some such development inspires us to concert our action with skill. (*Mein Kampf*, pp. 260–2.)

WYNDHAM LEWIS visited Germany in 1931, and immediately on his return wrote a persuasive book, *Hitler*, in which he said:

. . . in Adolf Hitler, the German man, we have, I assert, a 'Man of Peace'. . . . The Iron Cross, conspicuous upon his bosom, signifies that he is a brave soldier, not that he is a bravo or a pugilist. (p. 32.)

Hitler is *not* a straightforward, simple, fire-eating, true-blue, sabre-rattling, moustachioed puppet at all. I do not think that if Hitler had his way he would bring the fire and the sword across otherwise peaceful frontiers. He would, I am positive, remain peacefully at home. . . . (pp. 47–8.)

I am myself content to regard [Hitler] as the expression of current German manhood—resolved, with that admirable tenacity, hardihood, and intellectual acumen of the Teuton, not to take their politics at second-hand, not to drift, but to seize the big bull of Finance by the horns, and to take a chance for the sake of freedom. (pp. 201–2.)

SIR HORACE RUMBOLD wrote privately from Berlin on 30 April 1932:

Hitler himself may be described as a Revivalist preacher with the appearance of a greengrocer wearing an Air Force moustache. The material around him is very poor, and his principal lieutenant at Berlin is a demagogue of the first water, who denounces Jews and rich people generally as persons who, after oppressing the poor, go home and eat caviare in spoonfuls. (Unpublished letter, Rumbold Papers.)

In 1938 LORD LONDONDERRY reflected on Hitler's coming to power:

Herr Hitler restored the sense of national pride and self-respect. He carried out his programme in the face of the tremendous difficulties which had assailed his country—of being defeated, of suffering acute privation, of passing through various stages of political revolution, of having an army of occupation within the German frontiers for a decade, and finally of being disappointed and refused a fair hearing in the councils of Europe. On becoming Chancellor in 1933, Herr Hitler challenged these disabilities; and by his example and inspiration he inculcated in the people he was leading the spirit of self-respect and the desire for equality with other nations in their rights and responsibilities. (*Ourselves and Germany*, pp. 21–2.)

A perceptive British diplomat, FRANK ASHTON-GWATKIN, heard Hitler speak in August 1934, and commented:

Hitler himself looked well and young. He is not like his ordinary photographs or the impression given of him abroad. He does not look like either a fanatic or a poseur. He does not make a disagreeable impression. He is simple and direct—a man of the people, with no claim to the prophet's mantle or the emperor's crown.

He represents a new phenomenon, perhaps, among the rulers of this world. The 'little fellow' who has come into power because there are so many millions of him and because he has seen through the bluff of the 'upper classes' and of 'organised labour'. The 'little fellow'; who has ideas and ideals of his own, crude and half-baked perhaps, but with something in them; who wants his children to have more fun out of life than he has had; and who is therefore opposed to war—to civil war, class war, foreign war. He is opposed to exploitation. Work is good, and all should work; but it should be work that provides some pride and pleasure. Profit (or subsistence) should not be the only criterion. There should be leisure, and leisure reasonably employed under guidance. *Kraft durch Freude.*

If this is the basis of Hitlerism and of other parallel movements discernible in the modern world, it should be wholly compatible with world peace and progressive well being. Unfortunately the situation in Germany and elsewhere is complicated by factors of internal stress and of international rivalry and hatred which are likely to postpone indefinitely a peaceful solution and may possibly lead back to war. But Hitlerism is not essentially incompatible—as, for instance, is Russo-Marxian internationalism with its insistence on the class war and the cult of revolution.

But to return to Hitler as he stood on the temporary wooden tribune that dominated the hundreds of thousands summoned to applaud him on the heights of Ehrenbreitstein.

His methods were those of a revivalist preacher. He is something of a cross between a Salvationist and a Gunman. The sick and the aged were brought up to him for his blessing; even the little children, forbid them not, for of such also is the Reich of Hitler.

He is the antithesis of aristocracy; and it is difficult for us, who have been trained in the old schools, to recognise wherein and whereby he is the Führer. In the grotesque legend of German Knight errantry, we may see in him a Sancho Panza to the Don Quixote of ex-Kaiser Wilhelm.

His speech was clear and easily intelligible. There appeared to be no oratorical or emotional tricks. The emotion came from the crowd, which from time to time broke into apparently spontaneous ejaculations of 'Heil!', 'Heil Hitler!', etc.,—like the Allelujahs which greet Mrs Aimée Macpherson and her like—with a show of upraised arms that is unquestionably impressive.

So might the hordes of Clovis and Charlemagne have emphasised their unanimous loyalty.

'*Je weiser und mächtiger ein Meister ist, um so unmittelbarer kommt sein Werk zu stande, und um so einfacher ist es.*' [The wiser and more powerful a Master is, the more directly does his work come into being, and the more simple it is.]

I have just read this sentence in the works of Meister Eckehart, the medieval mystic recently acclaimed by Herr Rosenberg as the foundation of German wisdom; and it may point towards the secret of Adolf Hitler's personal predominance—the secret of which is not otherwise evident—directness, simplicity. (Unpublished document. Copy in the author's possession.)

LORD LOTHIAN visited Hitler at the end of January 1935, and wrote on his return:

I am convinced that Hitler does not want war. I believe that what the Germans are after is a strong but not an excessive army which will enable them to deal with Russia. . . .

Hitler is anxious to come to terms with us and I think trusts us . . . of course all the wolves of hatred and fear and suspicion are clamouring to prevent an understanding. (Unpublished letter, Lothian Papers.)

A year later LORD LOTHIAN's views were unchanged:

My view is quite simple. I loathe all the dictatorships. I think Mussolini and the Pope are the worst. I think after that Litvinov with his intrigue all over Europe to keep the European powers on the edge of war or to drive them into war is the next, and that Hitler, who is a visionary rather than a gangster, is by far the least evil of the lot. . . .

I think the Germans in themselves are much better people than the Italians or the Russians, and are much more likely to insist on recovering some measure of control over their Govt., once we cease the policy of persecuting them because it placates French terrors and pleases Russian aspirations. (Unpublished letter, 7 May 1936, Lothian Papers.)

LEO AMERY met Hitler on 13 August 1935:

While I found him shrewder than I expected, he certainly did not strike me as of outstanding intellect, still less as possessing a peculiarly impressive or hypnotic personality. In spite of his efforts to be agreeable I found him unattractive and, above all, commonplace—my first impression was that both his appearance and manner were those of a shopwalker. (*My Political Life*, vol. III, p. 130.)

ANTHONY EDEN visited Hitler in 1934 and recalled in his memoirs:

We were received in a vast room of *palais de danse* proportions, which we approached through many passages lined with guards and the trappings of dictatorship. Hitler had just completed his first year as

Chancellor. Smaller and slighter than I had expected from his photographs, his appearance was smart, almost dapper, despite his incongruous uniform. He was restrained and friendly. Though talking at some length when once he got going, he was always quite ready to accept questions or interruptions. I was told that he was quieter than usual. Certainly he listened to what I had to say at each meeting, waiting patiently for the translation. There were neither fidgets nor exclamations. . . . Hitler impressed me during these discussions as much more than a demagogue. He knew what he was speaking about and, as the long interviews proceeded, showed himself completely master of his subject. . . .

Hitler declared that Germany had no interest in aggression. The war had taught his country that it was easier to destroy than to build up, and this formerly militarist people now saw that peace ought to be the permanent state of mankind. For all I then knew, these sentiments might be sincere. (*Facing the Dictators*, p. 61.)

On 30 June 1934 an outbreak of butchery occurred which indicated just how Hitler could act when he wished to be violent. Hitler, who wanted the absolute loyalty of the German Army, slaughtered the leaders of his own private army, the S.A., in order to obtain it. The slaughter spread to others against whom Hitler felt he had 'old scores' to settle, including General von Schleicher, who had been Chancellor immediately before Hitler himself. This butchery, known as 'the Night of the Long-Knives', was a clear warning of Hitler's capabilities.

WINSTON CHURCHILL wrote in 1935:

What manner of man is this grim figure who has performed these superb toils and loosed these frightful evils? Does he still share the passions he has evoked? Does he, in the full sunlight of worldly triumph, at the head of the great nation he has raised from the dust, still feel racked by the hatreds and antagonisms of his desperate struggle; or will they be discarded like the armour and cruel weapons of strife under the mellowing influences of success? Evidently a burning question for men of all nations! Those who have met Herr Hitler face to face in public business or on social terms have found a highly competent, cool, well-informed functionary with an agreeable manner, a disarming smile, and few have been unaffected by a subtle personal magnetism. Nor is this impression merely the dazzle of power. He exerted it on his companions at every stage of his struggle, even when his fortunes were in the lowest depths.

Thus the world lives on hopes that the worst is over, and that we may yet live to see Hitler a gentler figure in a happier age. (*Great Contemporaries*, p. 268.)

Lord Halifax visited Hitler in November 1937. Chamberlain hoped that this visit would improve Anglo–German relations. ARNOLD TOYNBEE suggested ironically why Lord Halifax, who as Viceroy of India had successfully placated Gandhi, might think himself able to bring Hitler to reason:

Mr Gandhi and Herr Hitler were two hardly distinguishable specimens of the same species of foreigner . . . both of them superlatively exotic, and the average member of a British Cabinet may have reasoned in November 1937 that the guileless tamer of Gandhi had at any rate 'a sporting chance' of taming Hitler likewise. Were not both these political 'mad-mullahs', non-smokers, non-drinkers of alcohol, non-eaters of meat, non-riders on horseback, and non-practisers of blood-sports in their cranky private lives? (*Survey of International Affairs*, 1937, vol. I, p. 338.)

The meeting of Hitler and Halifax took place on 19 November 1937. According to the official German record LORD HALIFAX told Hitler:

. . . the great services which the Chancellor had performed in the reconstruction of Germany were fully recognized, and, if the public opinion of England took up an attitude of criticism from time to time towards certain German problems, it might no doubt be in part because people in England were not fully informed of the motives and attendant circumstances of certain measures taken in Germany. Thus the Church of England followed with anxiety and disquiet the development of the Church question in Germany; and Labour Party circles were critical of certain action taken in Germany. In spite of these difficulties, he [Halifax] recognized that the Chancellor had not only performed great services in Germany but also, as he would no doubt feel, had been able, by preventing the entry of communism into his own country, to bar its passage farther west. (*German Documents* D, vol. I, no. 31.)

On 27 December 1937 LLOYD GEORGE, who had visited Hitler in 1936, wrote to a friend:

. . . I shall never forget the extraordinarily interesting tour which you organized for me and my friends in Germany last year, which I had the privilege of meeting the great Leader of a great people.

I have never doubted the fundamental greatness of Herr Hitler as a man even in moments of profound disagreement with his policy. . . . I have never withdrawn one particle of the admiration which I personally felt for him and expressed on my return from Germany. I only wish we had a man of his supreme quality at the head of affairs in our country today. (Letter quoted in *Tempestuous Journey*, by Frank Owen, p. 737.)

LADY LONDONDERRY had also visited Hitler. In February 1937 she wrote:

I was prepared to find Herr Hitler as he is invariably represented in our daily Press—a fierce, fighting type of swashbuckler.

But on our meeting I discovered that this impression was far removed from the truth. I was at once aware of an arresting personality, a statesman endowed with remarkably expressive and far-seeing eyes.

I realised that here at last was a man who possessed the greatness to be perfectly simple. . . .

He neither smokes nor does he drink wine or spirits, and he is a vegetarian. Nor, unlike the majority of rulers and politicians, does he touch a penny of his official salary. . . .

From the Führer's own lips I learned of the great desire which he has for friendship with the English. . . . Surely this offer of friendship merits acceptance in the spirit in which it has been made, instead of the rather suspicious view of our Foreign Office with its Gallic bias appears to take it. (*Anglo–German Review*, vol. 1, no. 4, p. 155.)

GEORGE LANSBURY, a leading pacifist who had also met Hitler, wrote on 11 May 1937:

He is as simple and clear cut as was Lenin, and sure he is right as was Lenin, and as determined to stand by German independence as Lenin for International Revolution. Most fanatics are sincere, but they make lots of trouble. Even so, a soft word, a tiny recognition of Hitler's position by diplomats, would make all the difference.

He is a very lonely man and has no spiritual background to fall back upon, except that he believes he has saved Germany and is determined she shall not slip back again. He is ruthless and quite cynical with everything that seems to stand in his way. He will *not* go to war unless pushed into it by others. He knows how a European war will end. He is a good conversationalist and did *not* monopolise more time than I did. (Unpublished letter to Lord Allen of Hurtwood, Allen Papers.)

C. E. CARROLL, Editor of the *Anglo–German Review*, commented, in June 1937, on these visits to Hitler:

The Lloyd Georges, Lansburys, Lothians, and all the rest of the distinguished little procession that moves between Berlin and London, return with the certitude that, right or wrong, Hitler means what he says. . . .

The dominant note of his speeches is the will to peace. In proclaiming it he does not confine himself to pious platitudes. His will to peace is reasoned and firmly grounded. Nor does he see any reason or purpose in war. He has no aims a war could satisfy. (*Anglo–German Review*, vol. 1, no. 7, p. 290.)

Carroll quoted Hitler's speech of 30 January 1934:

The National Socialist Racial Idea and the theory underlying it do not lend to the underrating or disparagement of other nations. (*Ibid*.)

Not all those who visited Hitler were impressed. On 26 September 1937 GENERAL IRONSIDE made the popular pilgrimage:

He came walking down to us in his long coat and I was at once struck by his vacuous-looking grin—one can hardly call it a smile—and his watery, weak-looking eyes. . . . I chatted for a minute with him in German. He complimented me and told me I spoke it like a German.

The man struck me not at all. . . . He made no more impression on me than would have a somewhat mild professor whom I rather suspected of having a drop too much on occasions.

I must say that I was disappointed. The man must have the stuff in him, but he didn't make any impression upon me. (*The Ironside Diaries*, p. 29.)

In 1937 G. WARD-PRICE pleaded for a greater understanding of Hitler (and of Mussolini) in his book *I Know These Dictators*:

This [popular] conception of Hitler as a grim political robot is far from accurate. Behind the forceful character which he displays in public there is a human, pleasant personality known only to his intimates. . . . There is a strong strain of sadness and tenderness in his disposition. The intensity of feeling that imparts such high voltage to his public activities makes him sensitive to private griefs. (p. 16.)

Fondness for children and dogs is regarded by many as evidence of good nature. This is a strong trait in Hitler's character. (p. 21.)

To law-abiding citizens the Nazi Government brought public order, political peace, more work, better-living conditions, and the promise, since fulfilled, to make Germany once more a great nation. (p. 117.)

It is too late to disarm Germany by force; it may not be too late to disarm her by friendship. . . . Criticism of the Dictators and their works leads nowhere. . . . (p. 252.)

STEPHEN ROBERTS, Professor of Modern History at the University of Sydney, wrote *The House that Hitler Built* in 1937. It was an influential book and took another view of Hitler's activities. Roberts and Ward-Price were equally well acquainted with Nazi practice. Both had met Hitler. Roberts came to a different conclusion:

The whole teaching of Hitlerism is to justify war as an instrument of policy . . . and there is hardly a boy in Germany who does not view the preparation for ultimate war as the most important aspect of his life. . . . Hitlerism cannot achieve its aims without war; its ideology is that of war. . . . Hitler has worked up Germany to such a state that the people are ready to accept war at any moment. (p. 363.)

In 1938 Britain and Germany settled the Czech crisis without war—a successful return to Great Power diplomacy which accepted as axiomatic the refusal to allow small nations to stand in the way of Great Power friendships. But many Englishmen felt that Hitler had been willing to use violence if his wishes were foiled. SIR NEVILE HENDERSON disliked the way in which critics of Germany made out that Hitler was mad. On 17 June 1939 he wrote to Lord Halifax:

From beginning to end the world has made the fatal mistake of underestimating Hitler. At first he was either a mountebank or a kind of Charlie Chaplin, an Austrian house-painter or inferior sort of Corporal and now he is a madman or a paranoiac. While in fact he is one of those extraordinary individuals whom the world throws up from time to time, sometimes for its ultimate good but generally for its immediate misfortune. If the word was already invented, I have no doubt but that Napoleon was described in London as a paranoiac just as Caesar was called an ambitious lunatic and liable to fits in Rome. It does not help to underestimate a man who is the absolute master of 80 million Germans and saying 'No' to dictators is not a policy in itself. (*British Documents* 3, VI, Appendix I (iv), p. 706.)

But after the German occupation of Prague in March 1939, few people were willing to defend Hitler. LORD LOTHIAN, who had tried to see the best in Hitler wrote to a friend on 18 May 1939:

In the last few months I have been driven to the conclusion that the organisation of resistance to Hitler is the necessary preliminary to a real settlement. I have recently studied the unexpurgated edition of *Mein Kampf.* (Unpublished letter, Lothian Papers.)

Immediately after the outbreak of war SIR NEVILE HENDERSON reflected on his experience:

We are not fighting about Danzig, or the Corridor, or what should be the line of demarcation between the German Reich and independent Czech or Polish republics. The shifting sands of Eastern Europe are not our real concern. We are crusaders, at war on behalf of Christian ideals *versus* pagan doctrines; to compel good faith and confidence in international agreements; to prove that aggression does not and shall not pay, and that war or the threat of war shall not be the main and final instrument of policy. These are not slogans or mere phrases. In the Germany of to-day, under the governance of Hitler and his fanatical Nazis, material power is alone worshipped, and she is claiming the right to seize by armed might and brute force any territory which she happens to covet, regardless of the will and wishes of its inhabitants. That is the plain and single fact. Had Hitler stopped after Munich, co-operation with him would still have been possible, and the world might have ended by acclaiming his genius and by condoning some of the means by which he achieved his German ends. He may still be a genius, but by his cynical destruction of Czech independence, and by his unprovoked attack on the Poles, he has branded himself in the eyes of the world as that most dangerous of all menaces to humanity, a criminal one. (*Failure of a Mission*, p. 294.)

Czechoslovakia

Neville Chamberlain became Prime Minister in May 1937, and for nearly a year foreign policy—in which he interested himself more than most Prime Ministers—was concerned primarily with Italy, and Italy's adventures in Spain and Abyssinia.

In March 1938 Hitler annexed Austria, and the German problem—which had been almost eclipsed since the initial shock of Nazi methods in 1933—became dominant once more. Chamberlain did not see why Germany should be Britain's enemy. He realised that, as a result of her defeat in 1918 and of the terms laid down at Versailles, her grievances were not those of ambition or avarice alone: she sought equality—of status and of advancement.

For Chamberlain appeasement was a comprehensive policy of giving Germany her rightful place in Europe, and by so doing, to make her a contented and gentler member of the European community. Those that sought to 'appease' Germany did so, not necessarily because they feared German ambitions, but because they recognised those ambitions as just, and feared lest by thwarting them they might drive Germany to violence.

After Germany annexed Austria it was clear that her eyes turned upon Czechoslovakia, where there was a large German-speaking minority living along the German frontier in the Sudeten mountains. These 'Sudeten' Germans were divided in their own minds as to whether they wanted a large degree of autonomy *within* Czechoslovakia or annexation with Germany.

Konrad Henlein's *Sudeten German Home Front* sprung into prominence in 1935 when it won 62 per cent of the votes of the German-speaking electorate. KONRAD HENLEIN's views were clearly expressed in 1931:

We declare war to the death upon Liberalism . . . men wish to be led in manly fashion . . . We all know that an un-German parliamentarism, an un-German party system which divides our people into inorganic parts, will and must break down.

By inorganic parts Henlein referred among others, to the Social Democrats, in whose ranks Czechs, Jews and Germans were mixed.

For Henlein the aim was an exclusive German group. In Prague, in 1936, he said:

As Germans in the Sudeten provinces . . . we feel ourselves as members of the great cultural community of Germans in the whole world, and have here, as we have always had, German cultural tasks to carry out characteristically.

But where those tasks included Jew-baiting, for example, they were not applauded by all Sudeten Germans.

British opinion was divided. Those who suspected Germany of being determined on villainy wanted to defend Czechoslovakia if she were attacked, and refused to believe that the Sudeten Germans (many of whom they knew were democrats, socialists and Jews) wished to be joined to the Germany of anti-semitic legislation, Nazi dictatorship, and much greater restriction on individual libery than obtained in Czechoslovakia. Czech treatment of Sudeten Germans was often unsympathetic; but it was in no sense as bad as Nazi German treatment of their opponents.

Neville Chamberlain was convinced, as were those who supported and advised him, that if Britain could take the initiative in the Czech question, and seek to persuade the Czechs to give the Sudetens full autonomy, or even let them join Germany, this gesture of British goodwill would convince Hitler that he had nothing to fear from Britain and that he could rely on Britain to satisfy his other outstanding claims in a calm, peaceful atmosphere.

On 13 March 1938 Germany annexed Austria. While, to some, this action appeared as a natural union of one German group to another, others feared that the annexation was a prelude to further German expansion.

LEO AMERY told the House of Commons on 14 March:

We must no longer go on drifting or halting between inconsistent policies. We must have a clear-cut policy one way or the other, or we shall certainly end in war. Austria collapsed because she was not prepared to fight. We all know that Czechoslovakia will fight. What are we going to do about that? One thing that will mean war is for us to go on hovering, half encouraging Czechoslovakia, half encouraging France with the idea that we stand behind her, half encouraging Germany to think that we shall run out. Let us either make up our minds that we must stand out, and let everybody concerned know it, or let us say to France, Czechoslovakia and Germany, in language as plain and simple as we can make it, that the first German soldier or aeroplane to cross the Czech border will bring the whole might of this country against Germany. (*Hansard.*)

On 16 March NEVILLE CHAMBERLAIN deprecated the idea of warning Germany not to use force, and of Britain threatening counter-force:

. . . there is no need to assume the use of force, or, indeed, to talk about it. Such talk is to be strongly deprecated. Not only can it do no good; it is bound to do harm. It must interfere with the progress of diplomacy, and it must increase feelings of insecurity and uncertainty. (*Hansard.*)

SIR ARCHIBALD SINCLAIR wrote to Lord Allen of Hurtwood on 22 March 1938:

I entirely agree that we must counsel moderation and even generosity at Prague, and fortunately the Czechs have never shown themselves deficient in those qualities. I find few things less easy to bear than the failure of some of our friends to realise how far the Czechs have gone and are willing to go to remove any legitimate grievances on the part of the German minority. (Unpublished letter, Allen Papers.)

On 24 March NEVILLE CHAMBERLAIN told the House of Commons that he opposed any specific guarantee to Czechoslovakia:

. . . should we at once declare our readiness to take military action in resistance to any forcible interference with the independence and integrity of Czechoslovakia . . .? . . . the suggested guarantee would apply irrespective of the circumstances by which it was brought into operation, and over which His Majesty's Government might not have been able to exercise any control. This position is not one that His Majesty's Government could see their way to accept. . . . His Majesty's Government feel themselves unable to give the prior guarantees suggested . . .

For their part, His Majesty's Government will at all times be ready to render any help in their power, by whatever means might seem most appropriate, towards the solution of questions likely to cause difficulty between the German and Czechoslovak Governments . . .

We still intend to employ ourselves, and to urge others to employ, the methods of reason and diplomacy rather than those of menace and force. (*Hansard.*)

SIR NEVILE HENDERSON explained his views on the Sudeten question to Lord Halifax, in a letter from Berlin on 7 April 1938:

We cannot win the battle for the rule of right versus might, unless and until our own moral position is unassailable.

I feel this very strongly about the Sudeten question. Living as they do in solid blocks on the German frontier they have, in my opinion, a moral right at least to self-administration and eventually to self-determination. It is morally unjust to compel this solid Teuton minority to remain subjected to a Slav central government at Prague . . .

I do believe that, once the Sudeten question is satisfactorily settled Hitler would be quite willing to talk seriously about disarmament . . .

I am not quite sure that he [Hitler] would spurn our good offices if they were on the basis of Federation of a sort in Czechoslovakia and of the ultimate right of self-determination . . .

If you could persuade Beneš[1] to agree in principle a solution on the above basis, I could easily and discreetly sound Hitler, through Ribbentrop, on the subject. (*British Documents* 3, I, Appendix I.)

While critics of appeasement wanted to proclaim, strongly and irrevocably, Britain's determination to fight for Czechoslovakia if Czechoslovakia were attacked by Germany, CHAMBERLAIN explained what it was that he sought to avoid:

Our policy is not one of dividing Europe into two opposing *blocs* of countries, each arming against the other amidst a growing flood of ill-will on both sides, which can only end in war. That seems to us to be a policy which is dangerous and stupid. You may say we may not approve of dictatorships . . . We cannot remove them. We have to live with them . . . We should take any and every opportunity to try to remove any genuine and legitimate grievance that may exist. (House of Commons, 8 April 1938.)

Henlein visited London privately between 12 and 14 May. He met, among others, Sir Archibald Sinclair, Sir Robert Vansittart and Winston Churchill. HENLEIN outlined his plan for the Sudetens:

(1) A central Parliament in Prague should deal with foreign policy, defence, finance and communications;
(2) All parties should be free to express their views and the Government should act on majority decisions;

---

[1] Eduard Beneš, President of Czechoslovakia.

(3) The frontier fortresses should be manned by Czech troops;
(4) The Sudeten German regions . . . should have local autonomy, i.e. their own town and county councils and a Diet for the debate of strictly regional matters;
(5) The tracing of the boundary and other factual matters might be left to an impartial tribunal, perhaps even appointed by the League of Nations . . . (*Survey of International Affairs 1938*, vol. 2, p. 117.)

At Breslau on 25 July HENLEIN re-iterated:

Nothing short of full autonomy will be acceptable to us. . . . We do not ask for annexation to the German Reich. (*Daily Telegraph*, 26 July 1938.)

On 17 May 1938 LORD ALLEN OF HURTWOOD wrote to Arnold Toynbee:

I am putting completely on one side my pacifist opinions, and am assuming that force must be put behind law in a world which remains armed. With that premise, my point is that to uphold under every conceivable circumstance the rule of law at a time when there is such a huge margin of doubt as to the capacity of material forces to maintain the law is terribly serious . . .

Unless force is overwhelming I think one then has to choose between two evils—the evil of a catastrophe in trying to uphold law—and the evil of allowing temporary casualties in morality. It is for that reason that I am willing to take the risks with morality during the transitional period in the hope—perhaps a vain one—that events will play into our hands. (Unpublished letter, Allen Papers.)

From Berlin, SIR NEVILE HENDERSON continued to urge the British Government to take the initiative in the Czech crisis. He wrote to Lord Halifax on 18 July:

. . . the Germans are losing or have lost faith in the efficacy of our intervention . . .

I honestly believe that the moment has come for Prague to get a real twist of the screw. . . . It is the French job, but if they won't face it I believe that we shall have to. (*British Documents* 3, I, no. 512.)

Two days later HENDERSON wrote to Sir Alexander Cadogan:

Beneš is no statesman or he would have seen the writing on the wall long ago. But I fear that the Czechs as a whole are an incorrigibly pigheaded people. (*British Documents* 3, I, no. 524.)

HENDERSON was persistent in pressing his views. On 22 July he wrote again to Cadogan:

It is easy to say but impossible to prove that Germany does not desire a settlement. . . . It is also easy for Dr Beneš to attribute all ill-faith and all difficulties to Germans and Sudetens, but I fancy that strict impartiality would distribute blame fairly equally. Certainly . . . extremists are not confined to one side of the frontier—or of any frontier, *vide* . . . the Jews and Communists everywhere . . .

I have never advocated a plebiscite except as a threat to induce the Czechoslovak Government to go to the limit of concessions, but I submit that it should now be definitely considered . . .

There can never be appeasement in Europe so long as Czechoslovakia remains the link with Moscow and hostile to Germany. Czechoslovakia can never enjoy a moment's peace so long as she remains the enemy of Germany. It is a case of the inexorable logic of geographical position. If she wants to survive at all she must come economically within the orbit of Germany. We poor mortals can kick against logic but we can never prevail against it in the end. (*British Documents* 3, 1, no. 534.)

On 26 July CHAMBERLAIN told the House of Commons:

If only we could find some peaceful solution of this Czechoslovakian question, I should myself feel that the way was open again for a further effort for a general appeasement—an appeasement which cannot be obtained until we can be satisfied that no major cause of difference or dispute remains unsettled. We have already demonstrated the possibility of complete agreement between a democratic and a totalitarian State, and I do not myself see why that experiment should not be repeated. . . . [The Anglo-German Naval Treaty] stands as a demonstration that it is possible for Germany and ourselves to agree upon matters which are vital to both of us . . .

I do not think that we ought to find it impossible to continue our efforts at understanding, which, if they were successful, would do so much to bring back confidence. (*Hansard.*)

During the same debate JOSIAH WEDGWOOD criticised Government policy:

A Sudeten area, given autonomy, given control of the police, will be ruled by the Nazi party in Germany . . . we have only to see what they have done with Danzig to realise what must be the inevitable end of any autonomous area handed over to the rule of the Nazi party. . . .

What have the Jews to gain, the Jews who have fled from the surrounding Reich into Czechoslovakia and are trying there to build up again a life for themselves? Directly Nazi rule comes along what happened in Austria will be repeated in the Sudeten Deutsch territory—another 20,000 suicides, another great tragedy . . . Every time you sacrifice one of your potential allies to this pathetic desire to appease the tyrants you merely bring nearer and make more inevitable that war which you pretend you are trying to avoid. (*Hansard.*)

Lord Runciman was sent to Czechoslovakia early in August to mediate between Czechs and Sudetens. He persuaded President Beneš to offer the Sudetens a large measure of autonomy within the framework of the Czech state. On 4 September Beneš produced his most comprehensive scheme—Plan No. 4—which met almost all the Sudeten demands.

Although the Sudetens were not asking to be joined to Germany, and although Hitler himself had not claimed the Sudeten areas, THE TIMES stated on 7 September:

If the Sudetens now ask for more than the Czech Government are ready to give in their latest set of proposals, it can only be inferred that the Germans are going beyond the mere removal of disabilities for those who do not find themselves at ease within the Czechoslovak Republic. In that case it might be worth while for the Czechoslovak Government to consider whether they should exclude altogether the project, which has found favour in some quarters, of making Czechoslovakia a more homogeneous state by the cession of that fringe of alien populations who are contiguous to the nation to which they are united by race. (*The Times*, 7 September 1938.)

Many people asked—in what quarters had the annexation proposal 'found favour'? As *The Times* was regarded as the almost official organ of the Government, it was assumed that Chamberlain favoured annexation. Although the Foreign Office issued a denial that annexation was the Government's policy, rumour persisted that Chamberlain was prepared to advocate it, and also, said some, to put pressure on Czechoslovakia to hand over the Sudeten areas.

On 12 September Hitler, in a violent speech, attacked Czech dishonesty, and demanded the right of 'self-determination' for the Sudetens. Prompted by this new patronage, Henlein rejected Beneš's Plan No. 4 on 13 September. The Runciman Mission, which had so nearly been successful, which had persuaded the Czechs to make wide-ranging proposals, and had almost convinced the Sudetens of the

wisdom of accepting them, thus failed because Hitler had at last intervened. Runciman left Prague on 15 September.

There seemed suddenly the danger that Hitler would force the issue
by invasion. Chamberlain therefore decided to attempt to solve the
Czech crisis by personal contact with Hitler. He would show Hitler
that Britain, far from encouraging the Czechs to resist, would in fact
put pressure on them to make whatever concessions Hitler demanded.

On 15 September Chamberlain flew to Munich—the first flight he
had ever made—and was driven to Hitler's 'lair' at Berchtesgaden. He
had with him, not the Chief Diplomatic Adviser, Sir Robert Vansittart,
but the Chief Industrial Adviser, Sir Horace Wilson.

Hitler asked Chamberlain whether he would accept self-determination for the Sudeten Germans. Chamberlain replied that he agreed in
principle, but would have to consult his Cabinet.

Chamberlain returned to London, and on 16 September told the
Cabinet of the position. LORD RUNCIMAN wa scalled in, and gave his
opinion (later published in the form of a letter dated 21 September):

Responsibility for the final break must, in my opinion, rest upon Herr
Henlein and Herr Frank and upon those of their supporters inside and
outside the country who were luring them to extreme and unconstitu-
tional action.

I have much sympathy, however, with the Sudeten case. It is a hard
thing to be ruled by an alien race; and I have been left with the impression that Czechoslovak rule in the Sudeten areas for the last twenty
years, though not actually oppressive and certainly not 'terroristic', has
been marked by tactlessness, lack of understanding, petty intolerance
and discrimination . . .

I consider, therefore, that these frontier districts [where the Sudeten
population is an important majority] should at once be transferred
from Czechoslovakia to Germany . . . (Quoted in full in *Munich:
Prologue to Tragedy* by J. Wheeler-Bennett, Appendix D.)

WHEELER-BENNETT commented:

. . . when Lord Runciman and his colleagues left Prague on September
16, no one had even suggested the transfer of Czech territory to Germany without a plebiscite. The *Sudeten–Deutsche Partei* had never made
such a demand, and Hitler himself on September 12 had confined his
demands to 'self-determination'. Indeed only in *The Times* editorial of
September 7 had this suggestion even been mooted, and the Foreign
Office had officially denied that these views represented in any way the
policy of His Majesty's Government. It would seem, therefore, that

either Lord Runciman, when in Prague, formed opinions as to the solution of the Sudeten problem which far outstripped anything that either Hitler or Henlein had then proposed, and that these opinions had immense influence upon the Cabinet, or that in the writing of his report he was influenced by what had been told him of the Führer's demands upon the Prime Minister. (*Munich: Prologue to Tragedy*, p. 112.)

The Cabinet accepted the principle of the transfer of territory; on 18 September Daladier and Bonnet, summoned to London, were persuaded to accept it, somewhat against their will. On 19 September Britain and France told the Czechs what terms they must accept. This was the first detailed proposal made by any of the Great Powers:

THE ANGLO-FRENCH PROPOSALS of September 18/19, 1938

1. We are both convinced that, after recent events, the point has now been reached where the further maintenance within the boundaries of the Czechoslovak State of the districts mainly inhabited by Sudeten–Deutsch cannot in fact continue any longer without imperilling the interests of Czechoslovakia herself and of European peace. In the light of these considerations both Governments have been compelled to the conclusion that the maintenance of peace and the safety of Czechoslovakia's vital interests cannot effectively be assured unless these areas are now transferred to the Reich.
2. This could be done either by direct transfer or as the result of a plebescite. . . . We anticipate in the absence of indication to the contrary that you may prefer to deal with the Sudeten–Deutsch problem by the method of direct transfer, and as a case by itself.
3. The areas for transfer would probably have to include areas with over 50% of German inhabitants, . . .
4. . . . His Majesty's Government in the United Kingdom would be prepared, as a contribution to the pacification of Europe, to join in an international guarantee of the new boundaries of the Czechoslovak State against unprovoked aggression. One of the principal conditions of such a guarantee would be the safeguarding of the independence of Czechoslovakia by the substitution of a general guarantee against unprovoked aggression in place of existing treaties which involve reciprocal obligations of a military character.

On 21 September CHURCHILL issued a statement to the Press:

The partition of Czechoslovakia under pressure from England and France amounts to the complete surrender of the Western Democracies to the Nazi threat of force. Such a collapse will bring peace or security neither to England nor to France. On the contrary, it will place these two nations in an ever weaker and more dangerous situation. The mere neutralisation of Czechoslovakia means the liberation of twenty-five German divisions, which will threaten the Western front; in addition to which it will open up for the triumphant Nazis the road to the Black Sea. It is not Czechoslovakia alone which is menaced, but also the freedom and the democracy of all nations. The belief that security can be obtained by throwing a small State to the wolves is a fatal delusion. The war potential of Germany will increase in a short time more rapidly than it will be possible for France and Great Britain to complete the measure necessary for their defence. (*The Gathering Storm*, p. 238.)

On 22 September, having obtained French and Czech acceptance to the transfer of the Sudetens to Germany, Chamberlain flew to see Hitler for the second time—this time to Godesberg, on the Rhine. Their conversation went somewhat as follows:

HITLER: 'Do I understand that the British, French and Czechoslovak Governments have agreed to the transfer of the Sudetenland from Czechoslovakia to Germany?'

CHAMBERLAIN: 'Yes.'

HITLER: 'I'm extremely sorry. But that is no longer of any use.'

Hitler now wanted other areas, not predominantly German, to be considered for transfer. After fierce argument, Hitler demanded total Czech withdrawal from the Sudeten areas by 28 September.

CHAMBERLAIN: 'But this is an ultimatum.'

HITLER: 'Nothing of the sort . . . look, the document is headed by the word memorandum.'

Chamberlain, according to his own account 'bitterly reproached the Chancellor for his failure to respond in any way to the efforts which I had made to secure peace'. Hitler then agreed to postpone his time limit to 1 October, and told Chamberlain: 'You are the only man to whom I have ever made a concession.'

Chamberlain returned to England to try once more to obtain French and Czech approval to Hitler's proposals, but a violent public speech by Hitler on 26 September, and even greater violence in personal interview with Sir Horace Wilson that same day, made it seem that Hitler was determined to invade Czechoslovakia.

The British Government produced new proposals. They realized

Hitler was concerned with the timing of the Czech operation, and therefore drafted a plan with a built-in time-table which they hoped both Germans and Czechs would accept.

THE BRITISH PLAN of September 27, 1938

1. German troops would occupy the territories of Egerland and Asch outside the Czech fortified line on October 1.
2. Meeting of German and Czech plenipotentiaries with a British representative at some town in the Sudentenland on October 3 . . . On the same date meeting of International Boundary Commission consisting of German, Czech and British members. On the same date, if possible, arrival of observers and again, if possible, British Legion . . .
   Duties:
   (*a*) to arrange for the immediate withdrawal of Czech troops and State police. (*b*) to lay down the broad line for safeguarding minorities in the ceded territories and for defining their rights to opt and to withdraw their property, similar arrangements being made for the German minority in the new Czechoslovakia. (*c*) to determine the actual instructions, based on the Anglo-French plan, to be given to the International Boundary Commission for the delimitation of the new frontier with the utmost speed.
3. October 10, entry of German troops into the zone in which the plenipotentiaries shall have indicated that their arrangements are complete . . .
4. The meeting of plenipotentiaries will have to consider whether further arrangements should be made for improving the frontier delimited by the Boundary Commission in October in order better to meet local geographical and economic requirements in the various localities. It would be for consideration whether local plebiscites would be necessary or desirable for this purpose.
5. As soon as possible negotiations to be started between Germany, Great Britain, France and Czechoslovakia, for the purpose (*a*) of arranging for joint measures for demobilization or withdrawal of troops, and (*b*) of revising Czechoslovakia's present treaty relationships and instituting a system jointly guaranteeing the new Czechoslovakia.

The Czechs at first refused to consider the British plan, but at last accepted it, after strong British pressure. A Four-Power Conference was at once arranged, and Chamberlain, Hitler, Daladier and Mussolini met at Munich on the morning of 29 September. The 'Munich Agreement' was signed in the early hours of 30 September. It was then sent to Prague, to Beneš who, confronted by this final proof that no one was willing to champion his cause, accepted.

The main terms of the MUNICH AGREEMENT were as follows:

Germany, the United Kingdom, France and Italy taking into consideration the agreement, which has already been reached in principle for the cession to Germany of the Sudeten German territory, have agreed on the following terms and conditions governing the said cession. . . .

1. The evacuation will begin on the 1st October.
2. . . . the evacuation . . . shall be completed by the 10th October . . . . . .
4. The occupation by stages of the predominantly German territory by German troops will begin on the 1st October . . .

The reactions to the Munich Agreement were mixed.

ELEANOR RATHBONE wrote to Canon Barry, on 30 September 1938:

I expect there will be great thanksgiving for peace in the churches tomorrow, and it occurs to me that it may be thought too much out of harmony with the general feeling to remind congregations or the Deity of so painful a subject as the Czechs. On the other hand, there are many people . . . in whom sense of relief is quite overborne by an agony of shame over the way in which the Czechs have been let down . . . those who feel like this, and who extend from the extremest Right to the extremest Left in politics, will feel it an added outrage if . . . there are no expressions of regret, pity and admiration for the magnificent coolness and courage shown by the Czechs and their Government. (*Eleanor Rathbone* by Mary Stocks, p. 250.)

Duff Cooper resigned from the Cabinet in protest against the Munich Agreement. Just as Chamberlain was deluged with letters approving of 'Munich', so equally Duff Cooper received thousands of letters and telegrams applauding the stand he had taken.

HAROLD MACMILLAN telegraphed to Duff Cooper:

MANY CONGRATULATIONS ON YOUR INSPIRING LEAD TO PUBLIC OPINION EARNESTLY HOPE MORE OF YOUR COLLEAGUES WILL FOLLOW YOUR EXAMPLE.[1] (Unpublished telegram, Duff Cooper Papers.)

[1] Duff Cooper was, however, the only Minister who resigned.

The historian A. J. P. TAYLOR wrote to Duff Cooper:

May I express my appreciation that in this hour of national humiliation there has still been found one Englishman not faithless to honour and principle and to the tradition of our great name? If England is in future to have a history, your name will be mentioned with respect and admiration.[1] (Unpublished letter, Duff Cooper Papers.)

Neville Chamberlain received 40,000 letters.

'In many [wrote Keith Feiling] the ruling feeling was that this had not been a stake . . . "that Britons should be asked to die for".' Feiling tells of 'the flowers and poems and umbrellas and fishing rods which rained in on Downing Street . . . Dutchmen sent their tulips; he received a request for a piece of his umbrella to make a relic in a Greek icon'. (*Life of Neville Chamberlain*, pp. 378–80.)

LOUIS MACNEICE described a third mood—neither gloom nor jubilation, but cynicism:

> But once again
>   The crisis is put off and things look better
> And we feel negotiation is not in vain—
>   Save my skin and damn my conscience.
> And negotiation wins,
>   If you can call it winning,
> And here we are—just as before—safe in our skins;
>   Glory to God for Munich.
> And stocks go up and wrecks
>   Are salved and politicians' reputations
> Go up like Jack-on-the-Beanstalk; only the Czechs
>   Go down and without fighting. (*Autumn Journal.*)

After the Munich Agreement had been signed, Chamberlain and Hitler conferred together. CHAMBERLAIN produced a Joint-Declaration, which he asked Hitler to sign with him. HITLER agreed:

We, the German Fuehrer and Chancellor, and the British Prime Minister, have had a further meeting to-day, and are agreed in recognising that the question of Anglo-German relations is of the first importance for the two countries and for Europe.

We regard the Agreement signed last night, and the Anglo-German Naval Agreement, as symbolic of the desire of our two peoples never to go to war with one another again.

[1] A. J. P. Taylor certainly bore this out in his own writing. In *The Trouble Makers* (1957) he calls Duff Cooper 'The hero of Munich'.

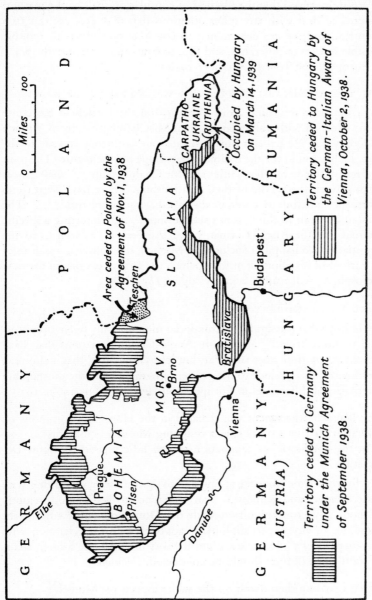

Czechoslovakia

We are resolved that the method of consulation shall be the method adopted to deal with any other questions that may concern our two countries, and we are determined to continue our efforts to remove possible sources of difference, and thus to contribute to assure the peace of Europe. (*The Times*, 1 October 1938.)

THE TIMES leader of 1 October 1938 was headed A NEW DAWN:

No conqueror returning from a victory on the battlefield has come home adorned with nobler laurels than Mr Chamberlain from Munich yesterday . . . He has not only relegated an agonizing episode to the past; he has found for the nations a new hope for the future. The joint declaration made by Herr Hitler and Mr Chamberlain . . . shall henceforth govern the whole of their relationships. There have been times when such a manifesto could be dismissed as a pious platitude. . . . The present, it is fair to think, is not such a time . . . By inserting a specific reference to the Anglo-German Naval Agreement, as well as to the negotiations so happily concluded at Munich, the Führer reminds us of an earnest of his good intentions, which the British people, in the new atmosphere, will readily acknowledge. (*The Times.*)

LORD LONDONDERRY wrote:

Let us hope that the signing of this declaration not only opens up a prospect of more friendly and secure Anglo-German relations than have existed at any time since the War, but let us hope, too, that it also may rank merely as a prelude to the greater settlement of all the outstanding international differences in Europe. (*Ourselves and Germany*, p. 163.)

The Munich Agreement was debated in the House of Commons on 3 October. DUFF COOPER, as a resigning Minister, spoke first.

In the course of his resignation speech he criticised the Joint Declaration:

. . . for the Prime Minister of England to sign, without consulting with his colleagues and without . . . any reference to his Allies, obviously without any communication with the Dominions and without the assistance of any expert diplomatic advisers, such a Declaration with the Dictator of a Great State, is not the way in which the foreign affairs of the British Empire should be conducted. (*Hansard.*)

DUFF COOPER then dwelt on the wider aspects of 'Munich':

I had been urging the mobilisation of the Fleet for many days. I had thought that this was the kind of language which would be easier for

Herr Hitler to understand than the guarded language of diplomacy or the conditional clauses of the Civil Service. I had urged that something in that direction might be done at the end of August and before the Prime Minister went to Berchtesgaden. I had suggested that it should accompany the mission of Sir Horace Wilson. I remember the Prime Minister stating it was the one thing that would ruin this mission, and I said it was the one thing that would lead it to success.

That is the deep difference between the Prime Minister and myself throughout these days. The Prime Minister has believed in addressing Herr Hitler through the language of sweet reasonableness. I have believed that he was more open to the language of the mailed fist . . .

The Prime Minister has confidence in the goodwill and in the word of Herr Hitler, although when Herr Hitler broke the Treaty of Versailles he undertook to keep the Treaty of Locarno, and when he broke the Treaty of Locarno he undertook not to interfere further, or to have further territorial claims in Europe. When he entered Austria by force he authorised his henchmen to give an authoritative assurance that he would not interfere with Czechoslovakia. That was less than six months ago. Still the Prime Minister believes that he can rely upon the good faith of Hitler. (*Hansard.*)

NEVILLE CHAMBERLAIN followed Duff Cooper:

The real triumph is that it has shown that representatives of four great powers can find it possible to agree on a way of carrying out a difficult and delicate operation by discussion instead of by force of arms . . .

The relief at our escape from this great peril of war has, I think, everywhere been mingled in this country with a profound feeling of sympathy—[Hon. Members: 'Shame.'] I have nothing to be ashamed of. Let those who have, hang their heads . . .

The path which leads to appeasement is long and bristles with obstacles. The question of Czechoslovakia is the latest and perhaps the most dangerous. Now that we have got past it, I feel that it may be possible to make further progress along the road to sanity. (*Hansard.*)

CLEMENT ATTLEE spoke for the Labour Party:

. . . We have been unable to go in for carefree rejoicing. We have felt that we are in the midst of a tragedy. We have felt humiliation. This has not been a victory for reason and humanity. It has been a victory for brute force . . . We have seen today a gallant, civilised and democratic people betrayed and handed over to a ruthless despotism. (*Hansard.*)

SIR ARCHIBALD SINCLAIR spoke for the Liberal Party:

A policy which imposes injustice on a small and weak nation and tyranny on free men and women can never be the foundation of lasting peace . . .

Was it wise of the Prime Minister to tickle the ears of the groundlings in his broadcast speech the other night by talking of quarrels in distant lands between peoples of whom we know nothing? Ought not responsible public men rather strive to make people understand the importance to our lives at home, to our standard of living, to the employment of our people and to the protection of our liberties, of distant but important places . . . Gibraltar, Spain, Singapore, the Suez Canal, the Panama Canal are all very distant . . . The Khyber Pass is distant too and very far inland . . . Czechoslovakia is much nearer home, and my foreboding is that we shall yet live to rue the day when His Majesty's Government sold the pass of freedom in Central Europe and laid open to the march of Germany all the people and resources of Eastern Europe. (*Hansard.*)

ANTHONY EDEN, who was Foreign Secretary until February 1938 said:

War has been averted, for which the world is immeasurably grateful; but . . . at the cost of grave injustice to a small and friendly nation. Czechoslovakia was not even heard in her own defence . . .

. . . my plea would be that the Government should not embark on a policy that leads to a Four-Power Pact, and should remember that no Council of Europe would be complete without the participation of all Powers, great and small. (*Hansard.*)

GEORGE LANSBURY was the first speaker, after Chamberlain himself, to approve of the Munich Agreement:

I hear all this denunciation of Herr Hitler and Signor Mussolini. I have met both of them, and can only say that they are very much like any other politician or diplomat one meets . . .

You may treat with Hitler and Mussolini how you may but in the end the only way that will win peace is to show reasonableness. The only way to combat evil is to set something better against it. Hatred is a destroyer. Vengeance brings its own evil reward. Love is the only thing that is eternal, because it is constructive. (*Hansard.*)

VICTOR RAIKES spoke for Conservative back-benchers who approved of the Munich Agreement:

If for a time war has been averted, let us remember that a war averted may be a war saved. Just as there have been criticisms passed on the

Prime Minister today, so there were criticisms of Disraeli when he came back from Berlin in 1874, yet that treaty kept the peace of Europe for 40 years. If by dealing with Germany, Italy and France on the present occasion we can maintain peace in Europe, not for 40 but for 30 or 20 years, it will have been justified. (*Hansard*.)

Hugh Dalton quoted a letter written by PROFESSOR TAWNEY to the *Manchester Guardian*:

Great Britain can still take the initiative, if it pleases, in building up a League of States who accept as their premises common resistance to aggression and the peaceful settlement of all disputes. That, on any long view, is the only way in which safety can be achieved and civilisation preserved. The ambition to be eaten last, which inspires our present policy, is intelligible but futile. We shall (if we remain edible) be eaten all the same, nor shall we be consulted as to the date of the ceremony.

The 'Munich' debate continued on 4 October. LEO AMERY spoke of the Czechs:

They may in the past have shown tactlessness and lack of understanding in dealing with their minorities. But they have not denied those minorities full cultural freedom, freedom of education, freedom of the Press and freedom of Parliamentary discussion. Of how many other States in Europe can that be said?

Can we really be so sure that Herr Hitler's genial pledges of last week will hold good against the urge for domination and the faith in armed force which are the very essence of the doctrines inculcated into every German . . . *Mein Kampf* has never let us down. We may pray for the miracle of a sudden conversion by personal contact, but dare we ignore the possibility of a back-sliding and of a reversion to type?

It was on the afternoon of 5 October that WINSTON CHURCHILL spoke:

All is over. Silent, mournful, abandoned, broken, Czechoslovakia recedes into the darkness . . .

I find unendurable the sense of our country falling into the power, into the orbit and influence of Nazi Germany, and of our existence becoming dependent upon their goodwill or pleasure. It is to prevent that that I have tried my best to urge the maintenance of every bulwark of defence—first, the timely creation of an Air Force superior to anything within striking distance of our shores; secondly, the gathering together of the collective strength of many nations; and thirdly, the making of alliances and military conventions, all within the Covenant, in order to gather together forces at any rate to restrain the onward movement of this power. It has all been in vain. Every position has been successively undermined and abandoned on specious and plausible excuses.

I do not grudge our loyal, brave people, who were ready to do their duty no matter what the cost, who never flinched under the strain of last week, the natural, spontaneous outburst of joy and relief when they learned that the hard ordeal would no longer be required of them at the moment; but they should know the truth. They should know that there has been gross neglect and deficiency in our defences; they should know that we have sustained a defeat without a war, the consequences of which will travel far with us along our road; they should know that we have passed an awful milestone in our history, when the whole equilibrium of Europe has been deranged, and that the terrible words have for the time being been pronounced against the Western democracies: 'Thou art weighed in the balance and found wanting.' And do not suppose that this is the end. This is only the beginning of the reckoning. This is only the first sip, the first foretaste of a bitter cup which will be proffered to us year by year unless, by a supreme recovery of moral health and martial vigour, we arise again and take our stand for freedom as in the olden time. (*Hansard*.)

HAROLD NICOLSON spoke later that evening:

There is the suggestion that Czechoslovakia was an artificial State, a fantasy of the Peace Conference. The hon. and gallant Members behind me [on the Conservative benches] did not call it an artificial state when they were using its armies to fight the Bolshevists. At that time it was not an artificial State: it was 'our gallant allies'; and gallant they were.

DAVID GRENFELL spoke bitterly of the so-called 'self-determination':

There has been no self-determination for Sudeten-Germans. Those Germans, as German as Herr Hitler himself, Germans of pure race and of pure speech, who do not agree with Herr Hitler in politics, have not been conceded the right of self-determination. Persecution, intimidation, assault, imprisonment—all these await Sudeten-Germans, to the number of 500,000, who have dared to be Social Democrats and not supporters of the Nazi régime. (*Hansard*.)

Hitler had been given the Sudeten districts of Czechoslovakia by Treaty; what remained of Czechoslovakia became thus less secure, and, having been deprived of both its mountain frontiers and its armaments factory, less able to resist any further aggression. The British Government appeared willing to guarantee rump Czechoslovakia against aggression; a guarantee that would be Britain's first firm commitment in Central Europe.

On 3 October 1938 NEVILLE CHAMBERLAIN told the Commons:

It is my hope, and my belief, that under the new system of guarantees, the new Czecho-Slovakia will find a greater security than she has ever enjoyed in the past. (*Hansard*.)

SIR SAMUEL HOARE said in the same debate:

I myself believe that the international guarantee in which we have taken part will more than compensate for the loss of the strategic frontier. (*Hansard*.)

SIR THOMAS INSKIP went further; he told the House of Commons:

His Majesty's Government feel under a moral obligation to Czechoslovakia to treat the guarantee as being now in force. In the event, therefore, of a net of unprovoked aggression against Czechoslovakia, His Majesty's Government would certainly feel bound to take all steps in their power to see that the integrity of Czechoslovakia is preserved. (*Hansard*.)

On 2 November the Germans and Italians 'awarded' Hungary the southern border fringe of Czechoslovakia. Neither Britain nor France were consulted. Another Czech frontier was destroyed. It might be argued that our guarantee should now come into force, but CHAMBERLAIN explained:

We never guaranteed the frontiers as they existed. What we did was to guarantee against unprovoked aggression—quite a different thing . . . Our guarantee was against unprovoked aggression and not the crystallization of frontiers. (*Hansard*.)

The guarantee for the new frontier of Czechoslovakia was never given; nor was any attempt made to rally the states of Eastern Europe into a definite alliance. Chamberlain wished to avoid the division of Europe into rigid power blocs. Others thought that Britain's own security lay in just such a division.

On 7 February 1939 HAROLD MACMILLAN asked the House of Commons:

Have we abandoned altogether the Eastern Front? Are we attempting to rebuild confidence and to bring together the smaller nations which are still looking for relief? They may be dominated today by Germany. What else can they do? They are not willingly dominated. We only need give them a lead in both financial support and trade. Leadership can still be given. (*Hansard.*)

But no British lead was given. On 15 March 1939 Hitler entered Prague, and the rump Czechoslovakia was made a German 'protectorate'.

On 15 March NEVILLE CHAMBERLAIN explained what had happened to the proposed British guarantee, which though nearly five months had passed since Munich, had not been given:

In our opinion the situation has radically altered since the Slovak Diet declared the independence of Slovakia. The effect of this declaration put an end by internal disruption to the state whose frontiers we had proposed to guarantee and, accordingly, the condition of affairs described by my Rt. Hon. friend the Secretary of State for the Dominions [Sir Thomas Inskip], *which was always regarded by us as being only of a transitory nature* has now ceased to exist, and His Majesty's Government cannot accordingly hold themselves any longer bound by this obligation. (*Hansard.*)

DAVID GRENFELL spoke up for the Czechs, and against Chamberlain:
I am very sorry indeed to find that on this occasion the Prime Minister has dismissed the whole problem of Czechoslovakia with such few words and with so scant amount of feeling . . . not one word of tribute to the Czechs fell from the Prime Minister's lips—not one word. . . . We have been told that the Government are trying to find appeasement. All that we witness day after day is a steady and violent disintegration of the European system, instead of modifying or retarding that disintegration, only gives an added impetus to it. . . . We have allowed the truth to be set aside, we have allowed violence to take the place of reason and justice, and violence has triumphed. A nation has been over-ridden and overwhelmed, and the rights of a nation have been deliberately set aside to pander to the hammer of force. (*Hansard.*)

SIR ORME SARGENT wrote in retrospect:
. . . it strikes me it is most unfair that the word 'appeasement' should have been debased to a term of abuse and condemned without any distinction being made between the many different forms that appeasement can take.

Many a time both in international affairs as in personal relations, appeasement is the only wise and prudent course to adopt to break an immediate deadlock and at the same time achieve an ulterior aim. It becomes questionable as a method of negotiation only if it can be shown to be *immoral*; i.e. the appeaser sacrifices the rights and interests of a third party and not his own when making his concession; or if it is clearly *dangerous*, i.e. where the concession made seriously undermines the strength of the appeaser either internally or internationally; this is especially so when the concession has to be repeated, for the appeasement then becomes nothing less than blackmail; and lastly when the whole process of appeasement is just *ineffective*; i.e. when the appeaser having to make his concession gets no quid quo pro in return.

In point of fact appeasement only stands condemned when it is proved to be ineffective. For if a position is really critical and if appeasement will bring salvation, we cannot be expected not to resort to it just because in normal circumstances it might have savoured of sharp practice, (necessity knows no law), or because it involves an element of risk which in normal circumstances we should not have been prepared to run. ('Out of this nettle danger, we pluck this flower safety.' Chamberlain said this of Munich and if only it had been true it would have justified his whole policy.) But if appeasement is ineffective it at once loses its whole raison d'être and becomes just a mug's game.

Our position at the time of Munich was, thanks to the Baldwin régime, such that we dare not condemn Chamberlain's resort to appeasement merely because it might seem immoral or because it was dangerous. It stands condemned solely because it was ineffective, because it was bound to be ineffective and because Chamberlain ought to have known it would be ineffective. He had only to study Hitler's technique—and he ought to have been studying it ever since 1933—in order to realise that Hitler would be prevented from responding to any sort of appeasement by his own temperament, by the political philosophy he had evolved and by all that he stood for in the eyes of the great and fanatical party which he had created and which was governing Germany . . .

You remember the famous passage in *Mein Kampf*—you probably know it by heart—when Hitler frankly and cynically expounds and justifies his whole method of political and military undermining. If Chamberlain did not know this passage or had forgotten it he showed criminal negligence. If he knew it and chose to ignore it, he was taking a criminal risk which cannot be explained away.

Besides, it was not as though the process of undermining had only just begun. It had been going on for well nigh five years and Hitler had proved the success of his method on at least three occasions; in rearming, in the reoccupation of the Rhineland and in the seizure of Austria.

When he launched his Sudeten campaign, he no doubt expected a protest as before followed by a grudging acceptance of the fait accompli. But I doubt whether even he expected Chamberlain to go further than this and in the name of appeasement to coerce the victim and thus legalise and underwrite the rape of Czechoslovakia in return for no thing more than that infamous scrap of paper.

If only we and France had not intervened, had sat back, had washed our hands of the whole business and had accepted under protest the final result, we should have done no more and no less than what we had done when Austria was seized; and we could have justified our inaction and soothed our consciences with the same arguments on that and previous occasions. We should at any rate have avoided the humiliation of going through the process of appeasing Hitler when we knew he could not be appeased, and mark you it was a humiliation, not because it was immoral, not because it was dangerous, but solely because it was ineffective, useless and a sham.

In saying this I ignore the excuse invented subsequently that Hitler gave us a year's grace in return for this our humiliation. It still always will be doubtful whether, this year's grace was of greater benefit to us than it was to Hitler and anyhow the argument is a dishonest one as is shown by the way the Munich settlement at the time was in all honesty and sincerity presented by its author to the British people as guaranteeing us peace in our time and the dawn of a new age of concord . . .

But although Hitler was not propitiated, I do believe that he was deceived by our servile act of abnegation. He must have interpreted it as proof that his method was succeeding even better than he had dared to expect and that we had reached quicker than he had anticipated the ultimate stage of demoralization which is the forerunner of complete capitulation. How could he, poor man, have been expected to understand that this grovelling gesture of ours signified on the contrary that the worm was at last going to make ready to turn? If he had realized this he might have hesitated in 1939 to make his next move as soon as was laid down in his timetable. Calculating Stalin too might have reached other conclusions than he did. But neither Hitler nor Stalin did interpret the Chamberlain intervention at Munich as a warning as they ought to have done, and so our act of appeasement far from delaying the war or enabling us to enter it in improved circumstances, may well have had precisely the opposite effect. (Unpublished letter, 30 December 1946. Copy in the author's possession.)

Britain and Russia

On 6 November 1917 the Bolsheviks, led by Lenin, came to power in Russia. Part of their success was a result of a pledge they made to stop the war, in which Russia had fought for three years as an ally of Britain and France. Leon Trotsky, in charge of Foreign Affairs, declared an armistice on all fronts on 21 November. On 11 December 1917 WINSTON CHURCHILL told an audience at Bedford:

Russia has been thoroughly beaten by the Germans. Her great heart has been broken, not only by German might, but by German intrigue; not only by German steel but by German gold. . . . It is this melancholy event which has prolonged the war, that has robbed the French and the British and the Italian armies of the prize that was, perhaps, almost within their reach this summer; it is this event, and this event alone, that has exposed us to perils and sorrows and sufferings which we have not deserved, which we cannot avoid, but under which we shall not bend. (Speech at Bedford, *The Times*, 11 December 1917.)

On 3 March 1918 Russia made peace with Germany at Brest-Litovsk, and ceded to Germany large tracts of territory and large amounts of war materials. The Allies took up positions on Russian soil, and, in August 1918, supporting the anti-Bolshevik Russians, attempted to crush Bolshevism by force, for they saw in it a terrible evil. JOSEPH KING, a Labour M.P., told the House of Commons on 16 May 1918:

The way in which the Russians have been spoken of in some of the great organs of the Press as if they were all traitors to the Allied cause, and as if they were all ready to accept so much money from the Germans or anybody else for any purpose, is offensive, and does absolutely no good. . . .

Of all the mistakes that are obvious there is none so great as our mistaken policy in the last few months towards Russia. (*Hansard.*)

The Government hoped that if the Bolsheviks could be defeated, a new Russian Government would come in, willing to join the Allies once more against Germany. LORD ROBERT CECIL, then Minister of Blockade, said in the House of Commons on 16 May 1918:

We have no quarrel with the Bolsheviks, but we wish to see Russia preserved as an Allied country, or, if that be impossible, as a non-German one. (*Hansard.*)

The intervention failed to restore Tsardom, or to bring Russia back into the war. The war ended, and Russia's support ceased to matter. The intervention had become unnecessary. No British Government could obtain support to continue the war for the purpose of destroying Bolshevism.

On 8 November 1919 Lloyd George announced that British intervention would end almost at once. WINSTON CHURCHILL stated at a public meeting:

No one knows what is coming out of the Russian cauldron, but it will almost certainly be something full of evil, full of menace for Britain, France and the United States. It seems to me therefore that our dangers . . . have not finally been removed by the war, and that, after a few years, they may come back again in a new, but still in a grave form. In order to prevent this we ought to try to make a real and lasting peace with the German people. . . . (Reported in *The Times*, 16 February 1920.)

In 1924 the Labour Government made a determined attack on anti-Bolshevik feeling. Britain announced her recognition of Russia on 1 February 1924, and on 8 August the Anglo-Soviet Treaty was signed in London. J. L. GARVIN wrote in *The Observer* on 5 October 1924:

The restoration of Russia to normal intercourse is essential to every purpose of the League, of disarmament, and of peace both in Europe and Asia . . . we regard the whole project as the best no less than the boldest attempt in Mr Ramsay MacDonald's Premiership. (*The Observer.*)

When the Conservatives came to power they refused to ratify the Anglo-Soviet Treaty. Not only Socialists but also Liberals criticised the Conservatives for what seemed a retrograde action. Philip Kerr (later Lord Lothian) wrote on 26 April 1925:

It is quite a mistake to believe that the present Government of Russia is a weak Government, liable to be easily overthrown. It is an exceedingly strong Government. Not only has it all the weapons of the State at its command. It rests upon very firm foundations. It rests upon the peasants, who regard it as the guarantee of their possession of the land as against the old landlords. It rests upon the industrial workers, who are now the privileged class. (*The Observer.*)

Conservatives, however, did not cease to criticise the Soviet Union. On 18 November 1925 DUFF COOPER told the House of Commons:

As to the internal government of Russia . . . There have been bad governments in Russia in the past; there have been none perhaps so tyrannical, so blood-thirsty, so oppressive, so anti-democratic as at present. . . . The chief difficulty in the way of our coming to reasonable terms with Russia and of persuading Russia to join the League of Nations, is the present Russian Government. . . . We desire Russia to join the League of Nations and to that end we sincerely hope that the present régime in Russia will shortly be destroyed. (*Hansard*.)

Hostility to Bolshevism led to conflict. On 12 May 1927 the police raided the offices of the Soviet Trade Delegation, and of the *Arcos* Trading Company. Immediately after the raid, the Government accused the Soviet Union of espionage, and, without bringing anyone to the Courts, or publishing any evidence, broke off diplomatic and trade relations with Russia. STANLEY BALDWIN said:

I wish, therefore, to state emphatically that our rupture of diplomatic relations does not in any way mean or imply War against Russia. The utmost it appears to mean is that we do not intend to have any further political dealings with Moscow. But we are wholly in favour of the pursuit of legitimate trade between the two countries. (Reported in *The Times*, 28 May 1927.)

J. L. GARVIN wrote in *The Observer* on 29 May 1927:

The raid by itself was a fiasco as regards the discovery of new and decisive evidence [of Soviet espionage]. But this being so, Parliamentary considerations forced the total breach in order to defend the raid. . . . Do we expect the Anglo-Russian question to remain simply in the air? And for how long? Have we no conception of what are to be the ultimate relations between the British and Russian peoples? And have we no considered view about the standing and irremovable problem of Britain, Russia and the world as affecting the prospects of the League, disarmament and peace? (*The Observer*.)

On 12 March 1933 six British subjects working for Metro-Vickers in the Soviet Union were arrested, and charged with espionage and sabotage. They were tried on 2 April; two were imprisoned (for two and three years respectively), three deported and one acquitted. On 19 April the British Government imposed a trade embargo on Russia; on 1 July the two men were released, and the embargo withdrawn.

The Metro-Vickers affair had further aggravated Anglo-Soviet relations. LLOYD GEORGE told the House of Commons on 28 November
1934:

... perhaps in a year, perhaps in two, the conservative elements in this
country will be looking to Germany as the bulwark against Communism in Europe. ...

Do not let us be in a hurry to condemn Germany. We shall be wel-
coming Germany as our friend. (*Hansard*.)

On 19 August 1936 the first Moscow 'purge' trial took place. On 25
August sixteen leading communists were sentenced to death, including
Zinoviev and Kamenev, who, after Lenin's death in 1924, had formed
with Stalin the ruling triumvirate.

Five months later the second 'purge' trial began, and on 1 February
1937 thirteen of the accused, all leading officials, were shot.

On 11 June, 1937 it was announced in Msocow that eight generals had
been sentenced to death on charges of treason and of spying 'on behalf
of an unfriendly state'. The eight generals were shot on 12 June.

On 3 March 1938 the trial opened in Moscow of another twenty-one
leading Soviet citizens. On 13 March eighteen of the twenty-one were
sentenced to death, including the Editor-in-Chief of the official Soviet
newspaper, the Chief of the secret police, and a former Ambassador
in Germany. Christian Rakovsky, former Ambassador to Britain, and
co-negotiator of the 1924 Anglo Soviet Treaty was sentenced to
twenty years penal servitude. He was then seventy years old. It is
thought that a number of leading British Socialists intervened with
Stalin to save him from execution.

As a result of the purges, British opinion became convinced that
Russia was weak and divided. The purge of the Generals, in particular,
seemed to point to a much crippled military potential. For many
people the purges served only to confirm the belief that Communism
was as brutal as Nazism. When, therefore, in early 1938, Hitler sought
the incorporation of German-speaking areas of Czechoslovakia into
Germany, many Englishmen were unwilling to take seriously, or to
approve, Soviet support for the Czechs.

The Russians attempted to interest Britain in a stand against Germany.
MAXIM LITVINOV the Soviet Foreign Minister, said on 17 March
1938:

The Soviet Government ... is ready as before to participate in collective actions, which would be decided upon jointly with it and which
would aim at checking the further development of aggression and at

eliminating the increased danger of a new world massacre. It is prepared immediately to take up in the League of Nations or outside of it the discussion with other powers of the practical measures which the circumstances demand. (*Documents on International Affairs 1938*, vol. 1, pp. 314–15.)

The Labour Party supported the Soviet initiative and urged the Government to take Litvinov's proposals seriously.

On 4 April 1938 NEVILLE CHAMBERLAIN told the House of Commons:

The second proposal . . . constitutes nothing less than a proposal for an offensive and defensive alliance between France, Russia and ourselves against some other Power or group of Powers. Is that what is called collective security? The party opposite never bother to look at the mixture inside the bottle, as long as the label outside is right. When I think of all their past fulminations against pre-war alliances, which they used to accuse us of wanting, I am amazed at their being able to bamboozle themselves into thinking that if they take a pre-war alliance, and mumble these words 'collective security' over it, they can change its character and the consequences that are bound to flow from it . . . the real effect of this proposal would be to do what we, at any rate, have always set our faces against, namely, to divide Europe into two opposing blocs or camps. So far from making a contribution to peace, I say that it would inevitably plunge us into war.

In the course of his speech CHAMBERLAIN said:

. . . the policy of His Majesty's Government, as stated [two weeks ago][1] has won the general approval of the whole country; and not only this country, but I may say practically the whole world, with the possible exception of Russia. (*Hansard.*)

SIR ARCHIBALD SINCLAIR spoke next, and replied:

The Prime Minister referred just now to the reception of his speech in the world. He said that it was everywhere well received, but added, with a note of contempt in his voice, 'except possibly in Russia'. What a fatal blunder. What a fatal blunder to refer like that to the great country of Russia, about which even 20 years ago Lord Balfour had the

---

[1] This policy was, said Chamberlain, to employ 'the methods of reason and diplomacy rather than those of menace and force'. House of Commons, 21 March 1938.

prevision to say, 'You must never leave Russia out of account when you are considering the affairs of Europe.' (*Hansard.*)

The British and French settled the Czech questions with the Germans and Italians. The Russians were not consulted. They appeared embittered by this. On 17 September 1938 PRAVDA the Communist Party newspaper, attacked Chamberlain for having 'refused to adopt the path of collective security against the aggressor'.

The strongest supporter of Anglo-Soviet co-operation—Winston Churchill—was treated as an outcast by Labour and Conservatives alike.

On 10 March 1939 JOSEPH STALIN spoke for four hours to the Eighteenth Congress of the Communist Party. Dealing with Foreign Policy he said:

Russia is in favour of supporting peoples who were victims of aggression and who struggled for the independence of their fatherland.

On 15 March Hitler occupied Prague, and Czechoslovakia became a German protectorate. The Russians at once offered to discuss a defensive alliance with Britain and France.

On March 26 NEVILLE CHAMBERLAIN wrote to his sister:

I must confess to the most profound distrust of Russia. I have no belief whatever in her ability to maintain an effective offensive, even if she wanted to. And I distrust her motives, which seem to me to have little connection with our ideas of liberty, and to be concerned only with setting everyone else by the ears. Moreover, she is both hated and suspected by many of the smaller States, notably by Poland, Roumania, and Finland. (Feiling, *Neville Chamberlain*, p. 403.)

On 31 March Chamberlain announced in the House of Commons a British guarantee for Poland.

SIR ARCHIBALD SINCLAIR spoke in the House of Commons on 13 April:

Some time ago the Prime Minister described himself as 'a go-getter for peace', and we all know how hard he has worked to justify that description. Now that he realises the necessity for building up resistance to aggression he must be a go-getter for friends and allies, and especially for Russia. He has much to live down. For a year he has held them at arm's length. For a year he has referred to them as a country 'half

European and half Asiatic' . . . it is not the right way to refer to one of the most powerful friends we can summon to our aid. (*Hansard*.)

In this same debate Winston Churchill urged 'the full inclusion of Soviet Russia in our defensive peace bloc'.

On 18 April 1939 the Soviet Union presented a comprehensive scheme to Britain and France. Lord Strang summarised the SOVIET PRO-POSALS as follows:

1. The United Kingdom, France and the Soviet Union to conclude with one another an agreement for a period of five to ten years by which they would oblige themselves to render mutually forthwith all manner of assistance, including that of a military nature, in case of aggression in Europe against any one of the contracting powers.
2. The United Kingdom, France and the Soviet Union to undertake to render all manner of assistance, including that of a military nature, to Eastern European states situated between the Baltic and Black seas and bordering on the Soviet Union in case of aggression against these states.
3. The United Kingdom, France and the Soviet Union to undertake to discuss and to settle within the shortest period of time the extent and forms of military assistance to be rendered by each of these states in fulfilment of paragraphs 1 and 2. (*Home and Abroad*, p. 163.)

On 4 May WINSTON CHURCHILL commented on the position in these terms:

Above all, time must not be lost. Ten or twelve days have already passed since the Russian offer was made. . . .

There is no means of maintaining an Eastern Front without the active aid of Russia. Russian interests are deeply concerned in preventing Herr Hitler's designs on Eastern Europe. It should still be possible to range all the States and people from the Baltic to the Black Sea in one solid front against a new outrage or invasion. (*Hansard*.)

Chamberlain was still suspicious of Russian intentions, and when a Communist M.P. suggested he visit Stalin, Chamberlain alluded sar-castically to the purges:

MR GALLACHER said:

In view of the statement made by Stalin that the Soviet Union is very anxious indeed to provide assistance for any country that is attacked by an aggressor, will not the Rt. Hon. Gentleman consider making per-sonal contact in order to get Stalin's own view?

NEVILLE CHAMBERLAIN:

Perhaps the Hon. Member would suggest with whom I should make personal contact, because personalities change rather rapidly. (House of Commons, 5 May 1939.)

On 8 April, Mussolini invaded Albania, and began to threaten Greece. When Chamberlain extended his promises of protection to Greece, LLOYD GEORGE declared, on 8 May:

Without Russia, these three guarantees to Poland, to Rumania and to Greece are the most reckless commitment that any country has ever entered into. I will say more. They are demented pledges that cannot be redeemed with this enormous deficiency, this great gap between the forces arrayed on the other side and the forces which at the present moment we could put in. (*Hansard.*)

The British replied to the Soviet proposals on 9 May, claiming that the time was not ripe for a comprehensive scheme such as Russia had proposed. Russia persisted and, despite a further evasive reply from Britain on 27 May, produced a Draft Treaty on 2 June. William Strang was sent to Moscow with the British reply, and negotiations began in earnest.

While the negotiations progressed, British politicians grew impatient. WINSTON CHURCHILL told the House of Commons on 19 May:

If you are ready to be an ally of Russia in time of war, which is the supreme test, the great occasion of all, if you are ready to join hands with Russia in the defence of Poland, which you have guaranteed, and of Roumania, why should you shrink from becoming the ally of Russia now, when you may by that very fact prevent the breaking out of war? I cannot understand all these refinements of diplomacy and delay.

LLOYD GEORGE spoke in the same debate:

There is a great desire, if possible, to do without Russia. Russia offered to come in months ago. For months we have been staring this powerful gift horse in the mouth.

WING-COMMANDER JAMES:

And seen its false teeth.

LLOYD GEORGE:

We are frightened of its teeth. That means that you cannot make up your mind; but the other people can. After all, you are not frightened of the teeth of those beasts of prey who have been tearing down one independent country after another. You are not afraid of them. We have pacts of friendship with them. We have been shaking *their* paws. (*Hansard.*)

ANTHONY EDEN also spoke:

I have never been able to see any reason why, on any part of the earth's surface, the relations of this country—the British Empire—and the Soviet Government should come into conflict. If there is one country that has surely got plenty to do at home, that country is Russia. One glance at the map is sufficient to show how vast are her territories, and travel in any part of Russia's giant distances reinforces that conviction, that no country in the world has a greater need for peace. . . .

I really cannot understand why we should hesitate to come to an agreement. (*Hansard.*)

The delay was, however, as much on Russia's side as on Britain's. LORD STRANG has suggested some of the doubts that may have been in the Russians' minds; and accounted for Russia maintaining her contacts with Germany while negotiating with Britain:

. . . were the Western Powers to be trusted? Would they not, having got the Soviet Union into a war, leave her to bear the German onslaught alone? (*Home and Abroad,* p. 196.)

On 23 July 1939 the Draft Anglo-Franco-Soviet agreement was completed—the only major issue unsettled was the military one, for which Military talks were to be conducted as soon as the British and French Military Missions could arrive in Moscow.

Article 1 of the ANGLO-FRANCO-SOVIET AGREEMENT began:

The United Kingdom, France and the U.S.S.R. undertake to give to each other immediately all effective assistance if one of the three countries becomes involved in hostilities with a European Power as a result either

(1) of aggression aimed by that Power against one of these three countries or

(2) of aggression, direct or indirect, aimed by that Power against any European State whose independence or neutrality the contracting country concerned feels obliged to defend against such aggression.

Agreement was nearly reached in Moscow: in London Anglo-Soviet cultural relations were improving.

On 19 June the Russian Ballet Company, directed by Fokine, began a month's engagement at Covent Garden.

There was some delay in sending the British Military Mission to Russia. On 31 July 1939 SIR ARCHIBALD SINCLAIR told the House of Commons:

We want the help of Russia. Therefore, we must dissipate the fog of suspicion and distrust of Britain which exists there. Therefore we must make friends with Russia, and the first principle of friendship is respect. . . . we ought to send to represent us . . . if only for a short time, a man of the highest standing in the country . . . a man who on account of his personal status and perhaps of the dignity of his office would have access to the most powerful authorities in the Kremlin. (*Hansard*.)

HUGH DALTON also spoke:

If the question is asked: 'Is Russia yet a member of this Peace Front and of this grand alliance against aggression?' the answer is—'Not yet.' Indeed, during these $4\frac{1}{2}$ months, much the worst feature, as it seems to me, and the feature which is most open to criticism, is the Government's very long delay in these negotiations with the Soviet Union. . . .
. . . it is no exaggeration to say that, could we be quite sure that Russia was all-in with us . . . there would be no war this year at least, and perhaps for a long time further into the future. (*Hansard*.)

SIR ARNOLD WILSON said:

I hope we shall not be required to sign the Anglo-Russian Agreement on the dotted line merely to be able to get an agreement. . . . Russia requires her forces to have access to and to march through the territories of both Poland and Rumania, who are likely to find such a prospect quite intolerable. (*Hansard*.)

LORD STRANG wrote in retrospect:

The British Government could not in honour disregard Polish (and Roumanian) susceptibilities. They had tried to find a way to bring the Soviet Union in without doing violence to Poland's interests. The question was: if Soviet troops entered Poland, even in Poland's defence, would they ever quit? This was a question which was never satisfactorily answered; and upon it the whole operation ultimately broke down. (*Home and Abroad*, p. 163.)

Unaware that the major obstruction came from Poland, Labour politicians were suspicious of Chamberlain's intentions. On 2 August 1939 ARTHUR GREENWOOD told the House of Commons:

... what guarantee have we that when our backs are turned the Government will not throw in their hands on this question of a triple alliance or arrangement between us and France and Russia? I am not saying they will do so, but I am saying that they might. (*Hansard.*)

On 12 August the Anglo-French military mission reached Moscow. The Poles refused to countenance the arrival of Soviet troops, even as allies and in transit, on their soil.

On 23 August the German–Soviet non-aggression pact was signed in Moscow, and Anglo-Soviet negotiations came to an abrupt end. The Pact was unexpected. M.P.s were shocked to realise that negotiations with Russia had failed, and tried to explain why.

On 24 August 1939 MISS ELEANOR RATHBONE said in the House of Commons:

When the guarantee was given to Poland, why was Russia not consulted first? Why was she not asked whether she would not stand by our side in giving a guarantee? I believe she would have done it at that time. It was the worst way to conduct these negotiations when the Prime Minister himself twice went to see Hitler, and took the Foreign Secretary with him to see Mussolini, but sent neither a Minister nor an Ambassador to Russia. The negotiations were conducted by a mere Councillor (i.e. William Strang).

GEOFFREY LE M. MANDER told the House of Commons that Anthony Eden could save the situation:

Does anybody suppose that if [Mr Eden] . . . had been sent to Moscow, as Foreign Secretary, two months ago, we should not have Russia on our side at the present time? . . . I hope that it is not too late even now for some step of that kind to be taken, possibly even by the Right Hon. Gentleman [Mr Eden] himself. (*Hansard.*)

GEORGE LANSBURY had an even more daring scheme:

If I were the Prime Minister I should write to Stalin or telegraph to him and tell him that I was going to see him as soon as an aeroplane could get me there. I know that there are people who all the time have thought that it was wrong to have dealings with the Bolshevists. But

I happen to have spent five hours with Joseph Stalin and I do not believe, and I shall not believe till the event proves it, that either Stalin or any other member of the Russian Government desires anything else but peace for Russia and peace for the world. (*Hansard.*)

On 1 September 1939 Hitler invaded Poland; on 17 September Russian troops occupied the eastern third of the country while the Germans completed their conquest of the rest. Britain declared war on Germany, for invading Poland, on 3 September. The Russian aggression was ignored.

On 22 June 1941, after less than two years of uneasy peace, Germany discarded the Russo-German pact and invaded Russia. Britain and Russia thus became Allies, for the second time within thirty years, pledged to defeat Germany. Though they had failed to unite against Germany either during the Czech or Polish crises, they remained allies long enough to see the defeat of Germany in 1945.

Poland

Like Czechoslovakia, Poland was a 'creation' of the Versailles Treaty. There was thus no immediate tradition of Anglo-Polish friendship. Poland's internal affairs were less savoury, to English eyes, than those of Czechoslovakia. SIR ROBERT VANSITTART wrote in his memoirs:

In May 1926 Pilsudski marched on Warsaw . . . set up his friend Moscicki as President, threw over the Left, banned communists . . . ruled for nine years and riddled the state with his creatures. Their poor quality antagonised not only their neighbours but the few British politicians who knew anything of Poland. A pro-Pole like Hugh Dalton was an extreme rarity. (*The Mist Procession*, p. 326.)

During the Czech crisis the Poles demanded, and seized, a portion of Czech territory—the mining district of Teschen. This move hardly enhanced Poland's reputation—yet Poland was possibly in great danger herself from German ambitions. During the 'Munich' debate, on 5 October 1938, HAROLD NICOLSON said:

At this very moment, as we are talking here, the countries of Europe, such as Bulgaria Rumania, Yugoslavia, which look to us . . . are probably drawing up trade treaties with Germany, thinking that now they have to make their terms. The tiger is showing his teeth; the cage door is open; the keeper is gone; . . .

. . . People abroad are going to say, 'This is the first time in the history of the British people for 250 years in which openly, avowedly and dramatically they have made friends with the strong as against the weak.' For 250 years at least the great foundation of our foreign policy, what Sir Eyre Crowe called 'a law of nature', has been to prevent by every means in our power the domination of Europe by any single Power or group of Powers. That principle has necessarily had the corollary that we should always support the small Powers against the strong. (*Hansard.*)

On 6 October 1938 NEVILLE CHAMBERLAIN explained his policy:

. . . there are really only two possible alternatives. One of them is to base yourself upon the view that any sort of friendly relations, or possible relations, shall I say, with totalitarian States are impossible, that the assurances which have been given to me personally are worthless, that they have sinister designs and that they are bent upon the domination of Europe and the gradual destruction of democracies. Of course, on that hypothesis, war has got to come. . . .

. . . I do not believe that war is inevitable. Someone put into my hand a remark made by the great Pitt about 1787, when he said:

'To suppose that any nation can be unalterably the enemy of another is weak and childish and has its foundations neither in the experience of nations nor in the history of man.'

It seems to me that the strongest argument against the inevitability of war is to be found in something that everyone has recognised or that has been recognised in every part of the House. That is the universal aversion from war of the people, their hatred of the notion of starting to kill one another again. . . . What is the alternative to this bleak and barren policy of the inevitability of war? In my view it is that we should seek by all means in our power to avoid war, by analysing possible causes, by trying to remove them, by discussion in a spirit of collaboration and good will. I cannot believe that such a programme would be rejected by the people of this country, even if it does mean the establishment of personal contact with dictators, and of talks man to man on the basis that each, while maintaining his own ideas of the internal government of his country, is willing to allow that other systems may suit better other peoples. (*Hansard.*)

But Chamberlain never met Hitler again—and although Englishmen continued to reject war, Hitler had other plans. On 15 March 1939 he occupied Prague. This was followed, on 23 March, by the annexation of Memel—a German Baltic city separated from East Prussia at Versailles. Rumour suggested a German attack on Poland to be imminent. NEVILLE CHAMBERLAIN acted at once; announcing on 31 March in the House of Commons:

I now have to inform the House that . . . in the event of any action which clearly threatened Polish independence and which the Polish Government accordingly considered it vital to resist with their national forces, His Majesty's Government would feel themselves bound at once to lend the Polish Government all support in their power. They have given the Polish Government an assurance to this effect. (*Hansard.*)

This was Britain's first commitment in Eastern Europe. It was given in haste, and in favour of a country as far away and as unknown as Czechoslovakia had been. Had Poland a better claim to be protected than Czechoslovakia?

During the 'Munich' debate, on 4 October 1938, SIR THOMAS MOORE had told the House of Commons:

It is said that we might have to fight Germany some time, though God forbid that we should fight a friendly and kindly people. . . . Hitler passes and his régime passes, and the world map alters, but it is the people who are destroyed. If we have to fight some time, and again I emphasis may God forbid, let us remember that the people of Germany are just as good, honest, decent and kind as the people of this country; but if it has to come, for God's sake let it be on a question of principle affecting us and the future of civilisation, a question affecting the well-being of man. (*Hansard.*)

Was Poland as important a question as Sir Thomas Moore thought it ought to be?

On 1 April, THE TIMES commented:

The new obligation which this country yesterday assumed does not bind Great Britain to defend every inch of the present frontiers of Poland. The key word in the statement is not integrity but 'independence'. . . .

Mr Chamberlain's statement involves no blind acceptance of the *status quo.* . . .

This country has never been an advocate of the encirclement of Germany, and is not now opposed to the extension of Germany's economic activities and influence, nor to the constructive work she may yet do for Europe. (*The Times.*)

According to the DAILY EXPRESS leader of 1 April:

There is no discordant voice anywhere save only from this newspaper.

The *Daily Express* regrets—

(1) That a guarantee should have been given which involves Britain in the concerns of Eastern Europe.

(2) That it was given without seeking and obtaining the approval of the Dominions and their concurrence in the obligations.

The *Daily Express* opposes the commitment to Poland.

DUFF COOPER wrote:

Never before in our history have we left in the hands of one of the smaller Powers the decision whether or not Great Britain goes to war. But there the decision rests today, with a handful of men whose very names, with the possible exception of Colonel Beck, are unknown to the people of this country. These unknown men can decide that the European war shall begin tomorrow. (*The Second World War*, p. 320.)

LORD STRANG commented in 1956:

Normally, when any grave new step in foreign policy is in contemplation, its implications, political and military, are thoroughly canvassed by Ministers with their civilian and military advisers. In the case of the Polish declaration, the idea seems to have sprung fully grown from the Ministerial mind . . . it was framed under impact of alarming reports about imminent German intentions in regard to Poland which were, in fact, at the time ill-founded. (*Home and Abroad*, p. 161.)

SIR ORME SARGENT wrote of the Declaration:

My recollection is that it was an entirely personal act by Neville Chamberlain, who was so furious at having been deceived so grossly by Hitler that he simply went off the deep end without consulting anybody—'Un mouton enragé' as the French saying is. (Unpublished letter to the author, 5 June 1962.)

NEVILLE CHAMBERLAIN'S mood of defiance continued. On 13 April he announced in the House of Commons that Britain would come to the assistance of Greece and Rumania, if either were attacked:

His Majesty's Government feel that they have both a duty and service to perform by leaving no doubt in the mind of anyone as to their own position. (*Hansard.*)

But Britain's position was far from clear. Several Cabinet Ministers were said to be in favour of forcing Poland to make concessions to Germany, so that Britain could avoid being drawn into a European war. On 25 April Nevile Henderson returned to Berlin, having been recalled to England after Hitler's Prague coup in March. The Germans at once told him how obstinate the Poles were in refusing to make concessions to Germany. Henderson agreed with the Germans. On 27 April CLIFFORD NORTON, Councillor in the British Embassy in Warsaw wrote:

We here are all rather appalled by the tone and substance of recent telegrams from Berlin. They produce the impression that our Embassy are falling for the Nazi propaganda stuff that Poland is a menace to peace . . . This is playing the German game and it is a very dangerous one. For peace cannot be ensured by *any* Polish concessions unless those concessions are made as between equals. . . .

. . . it seems to me most dangerous for Berlin to use the same language about Danzig as they did about Czechoslovakia. . . . If peace is saved it will be because Hitler is afraid of the war on both fronts simultaneously. . . .

British policy . . . seems to us exiles to be moving from strength to strength along slow but sure lines . . . But I earnestly hope that *no one* at home will be misled by false analogies, or temporary forgetfulness of recent events, or ignorance of the game of 'nerves' now being played in Europe—by thinking that we can *buy* even a short respite except at a great cost.

And if the cost were that of letting the Poles down . . . I do not think that any member of this Embassy could remain here. . . . (*British Documents* 3, v, no. 301. Letter to William Strang.)

Danzig was a strange issue on which to call a halt to Hitler. It was a city almost entirely inhabited by Germans, who had elected local Nazis to rule over them. Hitler sought to incorporate this Nazi pocket into Germany and to link it to Germany by a corridor across Polish territory. Poland feared lest, once Danzig became German, the Nazis would then demand other areas of Poland. As SIR NEVILE HENDERSON wrote on 20 May:

. . . the fate of the Czechs rendered the Poles still more alive to the dangers of their own position. The Sudeten concession had not saved the Czechs, and similarly any Danzig-Corridor concession might not save Posen and Upper Silesia. (*British Documents* 3, v, no. 573. Letter to Lord Halifax.)

Nine days later, on 29 May, HENDERSON suggested concessions that, despite his previous doubts, he thought the Poles would be wise to make:

Danzig is a German city and an enclave of some 400,000 Germans, and sooner or later Germany is not going to leave it outside the Reich. . . . The solution I would aim at would be . . .

The Danzig enclave to be incorporated in Germany as a Free City and demilitarised area.

The Corridor to be equally demobilised. . . . (*British Documents* 3, v. no. 664.)

If Hitler knew of British doubts about coming to Poland's aid he might consider it safe to attack Poland without fear of a reprisal. On 6 June THOMAS JONES met Adam von Trott, a former Rhodes Scholar, who was on the German Army General Staff:

The only political move which he believes might impress the Leader and make him treat G.B. as a more dangerous element would be the establishment of a comprehensive war-time cabinet now. . . .

The unexpected formation of a Coalition Government representative of our 'Warmongers' and of our Left . . . might convince the German Government that we cannot be relied on to remain passive and ineffectual. This he feels *might* stay their hand. (*Diary with Letters*, p. 437.)

But Chamberlain had no intention of bringing Churchill, Eden, Amery or Duff Cooper from the so-called 'warmongers', or Attlee or Greenwood from the Left into his Government. He might strongly dislike the developments of German policy; his dislike of his domestic opponents was stronger still.

LORD BRAND, the financier, objected to the growing anti-Polish feeling. On 28 June he wrote to Geoffrey Dawson:

One hears in various quarters that now that the Government have to face the consequence of their Polish guarantee, they may be hesitating. Heaven knows none of us want a war. But, if we have another Munich, then no one in the world will follow us, and Europe East and Central, must all line up with Germany. The Peace Front disappears with appeasement. I heard the P.M. a very short time ago sing a Paean of Praise in honour of Munich as a great success, so he may want another.

I believe the moment is to the last extent critical and that we ought to form some form of National Government. If that is impossible owing to the P.M. then the Government should be strengthened by bringing in Winston, who will make a firm stand and will be known throughout the world to be ready for a firm stand. As at present constituted the Cabinet seem either 'career' men or hopeless mugwumps. (Quoted in *Geoffrey Dawson* by Evelyn Wrench, p. 393.)

On 3 July CLIFFORD NORTON wrote to Sir Orme Sargent:

It is of course rubbish to say that the Polish Government is liable to be more extreme owing to our guarantee.

On the contrary we have given them the strength and confidence to be reasonable despite perpetual pin-pricks.

In the official acts and statements of the leaders of the [Polish] people there is a dignity compared with which the utterances of Goebbels (who got very drunk at Danzig) are the bawling of a guttersnipe. (*British Documents* 3, VI, no. 224.)

Early in July there were rumours that Hitler intended to secure the return of Danzig to Germany by force. LORD LOTHIAN wrote on 5 July:

If [Neville] would put Winston into the Cabinet and mobilise the fleet as soon as any further sign of action in Danzig begins, there seems to me to be a good chance of Hitler sheering off a major crisis this autumn. If he does this because he is not prepared to face a general war it will be a severe blow to the solidity of the Axis. . . .

But the least sign of wobbling or of desire for more appeasement at this moment would I feel sure let the whole thing off this autumn. (Unpublished letter, Lothian Papers.)

CLIFFORD NORTON wrote to Sir Alexander Cadogan on 10 July:

May I whisper to you that from the Polish point of view our record in protecting victims of aggression has not recently been impressive. We, too, have a record to live down. . . .

The Poles feel that they are really our allies, and we shall get the best out of them by treating them as if we felt it too. . . . There are plenty of interested parties going about saying to us 'Don't trust Beck' and to the Poles 'Remember Munich'. The only way we shall defeat this propaganda and diminish the risk of hanging separately seems to me by hanging together. (*British Documents* 3, VI, no. 289.)

On 21 July SIR ARCHIBALD SINCLAIR told the House of Commons:

There can be no shadow of doubt about our obligations to help Poland defend herself against any aggression against Danzig. But when does aggression begin? . . .

The parties of 'tourists' visiting Danzig have increased to the point at which it is estimated . . . that there are now 60,000 German troops and S.S. men in Danzig territory. A quarter of the Danzig frontier with Poland is reported to be fortified; and further sums to complete the fortifications have been voted by the Danzig Senate and are being obtained by confiscating the property of the Jews. . . .

. . . His Majesty's Government must tell us and tell Germany at what point the line is going to be drawn in Danzig. (*Hansard.*)

The Government made no statement about Danzig; but they showed some enthusiasm for their new ally by sending General Ironside to Warsaw to discuss Anglo-Polish military co-operation.

This troubled Hitler. On 11 August 1939 he talked with Karl Burck-hardt, a Swiss, and the League High Commissioner for Danzig:

HITLER:

. . . I want to live in peace with England and conclude a definitive pact; to guarantee all the English possessions in the world and to collaborate.

BURCKHARDT:

Then would it not be better to have a direct conversation with an Englishman? . . .

HITLER:

Language is too big an obstacle. I realised it last year. I understand a little English. I stumble over a few words of French. I had a hard and difficult youth, and was not able to learn languages. An Englishman who could talk German? They tell me that General Ironside talks it fluently, the General who went to Warsaw!

BURCKHARDT:

Could I pass on such a wish.

HITLER:

Yes . . . the matter is rather urgent. (*British Documents* 3, VI, no. 659.)

At one point in their conversation, Hitler told Burckhardt that he would 'annihilate' Poland.

On 11 August EVELYN WRENCH wrote to *The Times*:

Danzig today is a very different place from the peaceful city of 1927. In the Free City are now to be seen all the outward emblems of Nazi power: fluttering swastika banners, young S.S. men in their black uniforms, German policemen and motor-lorries full of armed men. . . . With the object lesson of Czecho-Slovakia in mind, is Poland unreasonable in demanding that her outlet on the Baltic be safeguarded? I do not think so. A week in Warsaw only confirmed the impression that the Polish Government is acting with great restraint in very difficult circumstances. (*The Times*.)

SIR NEVILE HENDERSON explained to William Strang on 16 August that the Poles were far from innocent:

. . . Warsaw with its civilized and intelligent, not to say astute clique with which one consorts there, is one thing: outside in the country the Poles are an utterly uncivilized lot. . . .

We would not say boo to Beneš last year, till we were on the abyss of war. And we can't say boo to Beck this year. (*British Documents* 3, VII. no. 37.)

GENERAL IRONSIDE returned from Warsaw, and on 23 August wrote in his diary:

This morning I get a message from the War Office to attend a conference for Commanders 'to discuss the present emergency'. It makes one quite sick . . . I told [Hore-] Belisha yesterday that he ought to mobilise . . . We have absolutely no direction from above and no signs of anybody with personality enough to direct. Pitiable at a moment like this. (*The Ironside Diaries*, p. 89.)

Hitler's threats against Poland were fortified by the Russo-German non-aggression Pact on 22 August. Britain now saw clearly that all chance of Anglo-Russian co-operation was ended. To emphasise that this blow would not weaken her resolve, she finalised her pledges to Poland by hastening negotiations for an Anglo-Polish Treaty.

On 25 August the Anglo-Polish Treaty was signed in London, giving a greater stamp of authority to Chamberlain's Declaration of 31 March. The Treaty re-iterated and elaborated the terms of the Declaration. In a secret clause it pledged Britain to support Poland if Danzig were seized by Germany.

HAROLD NICOLSON wrote in 1940:

I believe that he [Hitler] imagined that if he could reverse his whole previous doctrine and enter into alliance with Russia, the two Western Powers would immediately retire from the fray. He thought that by this tremendous diplomatic bluff, by this gesture of 'broadened strategy', he would be able once again to win a white war. (*Background and Issues of the War*, by H. A. L. Fisher, Harold Nicolson and others, p. 110.)

The Germans realised that Henderson was strongly anti-Polish, and produced, at midnight on 30 August, what they claimed were Germany's complete and final demands. They had not, as yet, been shown to the Poles. Henderson was favourably impressed, and passed them on to Halifax. The main points were:

1. Restoration of Danzig to Germany.
2. Corridor to be demarcated (details of southern line given).
3. Plebiscite in Corridor on basis of 1919 population.
4. International commission to police Corridor.
5. Gydnia to be reserved to Poland.
6. Danzig to be purely commercial city and demilitarized.

SIR NEVILE HENDERSON urged Halifax to put pressure on the Poles. One had to consider, he said:

Not only immediate present in which it is essential not to display any indication of yielding to Herr Hitler's threats but also future. If there is to be any genuine peace in future between Poland and her powerful neighbour grievances of latter which are not of Herr Hitler's making but national must be eliminated. In my opinion in order to achieve this end City of Danzig . . . must revert to Germany; there must be direct and extra-territorial communication between Reich and East Prussia; and German minority in Poland must be got rid of by means of some exchange of population. On no other basis can there ever be genuine and lasting peace between the two countries. No diplomatic compromise has a hope of surviving indefinitely. . . . I can only urge once more importance of Poland accepting at once proposals for direct negotiations. (*British Documents* 3, VII, no. 537.)

SIR HOWARD KENNARD challenged Henderson's approval of the German terms:

His Majesty's Ambassador at Berlin appears to consider German terms reasonable. I fear that I cannot agree with him from point of view of Warsaw. While to the uninitiated they may seem plausible the Polish Government will certainly regard them as an attempt to strangle her under the cloak of legality. . . .

If Poland submits to peremptory and humiliating [demands] she will have surrendered the principle that discussions must be on a free and equal basis and in no sense under menace or pressure. This is a vital aspect of Polish independence which His Majesty's Government are pledged to sustain. . . .

As to terms themselves . . . they are when stripped of legalistic language clearly calculated to undermine the existence of the Polish State. . . .

Any suspicion that her allies could possibly wish such terms to be taken as basis for negotiation might even drive Polish to offer resistance single-handed to provocations they have for so long endured with fortitude and prudence. (*British Documents* 3, vol. VII, no. 618.)

The terms which Henderson trusted, and of which Kennard was suspicious, were a bluff.

On 1 September 1939, at dawn, the Germans invaded Poland. All that day they advanced across Polish territory—while their planes began to bomb Warsaw and other large cities. Although Britain was pledged to come to Poland's aid 'at once', and with all the assistance she could provide, there was delay. Mussolini urged a conference; France wanted to accept. Britain warned Germany about her attack on Poland —but it was a weak warning, without any time-limit. Chamberlain and his advisers still hoped that negotiations might be possible, and an Anglo-German war avoided.

On the morning of 2 September WINSTON CHURCHILL wrote to Chamberlain:

The Poles have now been under heavy attack for thirty hours, and I am much concerned to hear that there is talk in Paris of a further note. I trust you will be able to announce our Joint Declaration of War at *latest* when Parliament meets this afternoon. (*The Gathering Storm*, p. 318.)

The German attack across Poland continued throughout 2 September. The House of Commons expected war to be declared on Germany that day. The Cabinet met in the afternoon and decided that a British ultimatum should be sent to Germany that evening. But the French still urged negotiations—and Chamberlain and his closest advisers still hoped that Mussolini would persuade Hitler to halt his troops, and discuss his demands around a conference table. Shortly after 7.30 in the evening Chamberlain entered the House of Commons. All the M.P.s, and most of his Cabinet colleagues, expected that he would announce that Britain's ultimatum had been sent.

NEVILLE CHAMBERLAIN told the House of Commons:

His Majesty's Government will, as stated yesterday, be bound to take action unless the German forces are withdrawn from Polish territory. They are in communication with the French Government as to the limit of time within which it would be necessary for the British and French Governments to know whether the German Government were prepared to effect such a withdrawal. *If the German Government should agree to withdraw their forces then His Majesty's Government would be willing to regard the position as being the same as it was before the German forces crossed the Polish frontier.* That is to say, the way would be open to discussion between the German and Polish Governments on the matters at issue between them. (*Hansard.*)

LEO AMERY wrote in retrospect:

The House was aghast. For two whole days the wretched Poles had been bombed and massacred, and we were still considering within what time-limit Hitler should be invited to tell us whether he felt like relinquishing his prey! And then these sheer irrelevancies about the terms of a hypothetical agreement between Germany and Poland . . . Was all this havering the prelude to another Munich? A year before the House had risen to its feet to give Chamberlain an ovation when he announced a last-moment hope of peace. This time any similar announcement would have been met by a universal howl of execration. (*My Political Life*, vol. III, p. 324.)

According to DUFF COOPER, Chamberlain's statement—
... gave the impression that even at this late hour Great Britain was going to repeat the surrender of Munich. (*Old Men Forget*, p. 259.)

HUGH DALTON wrote in his diary:
In the Lobbies afterwards there was a terrific buzz. It almost seemed that, on a free vote, Chamberlain and Simon would have been overthrown. (*The Fateful Years*, p. 265.)

ARTHUR GREENWOOD spoke for the Labour Party—to Amery's cry of SPEAK FOR *ENGLAND*:
... I believe the whole House is perturbed by the Right Hon. Gentleman's statement. ...

Tomorrow we meet at twelve. I hope the Prime Minister then—well, he must be in a position to make some further statement—[Hon. Members: 'definite']—And I must put this point to him. Every minute's delay now means the loss of life, imperilling of our national interests——

ROBERT BOOTHBY:
'Honour.'

ARTHUR GREENWOOD:
Let me finish my sentence. I was about to say imperilling the very foundations of our national honour, and I hope, therefore, that tomorrow morning ... we shall know the mind of the British Government, and that there shall be no more devices for dragging out what has been dragged out too long. The moment we look like weakening, at that moment dictatorship knows we are beaten. (*Hansard.*)

Chamberlain could not ignore the pressure of Parliamentary opinion. A group of Cabinet Ministers told him, immediately after the Debate, that war must be declared, and all hope of further delay abandoned. The mood of Parliament was unmistakable.

A loyal Conservative back-bencher, SIR JOHN WARDLAW-MILNE, voiced the fears that troubled Conservatives, Socialists and Liberals:
... now it is ... 38 hours since this war began ... 24 hours ... since the Prime Minister's message was delivered in Germany ... I do pray

that he will remember . . . that the whole country is nervous about this continual delay in carrying out our pledges. (*Hansard.*)

NEVILLE CHAMBERLAIN telephoned Edouard Daladier and told him that:

. . . the question here was very grave. There had been an angry scene in the House of Commons after he had made his statement. . . . His colleagues in the Cabinet were also disturbed. . . . If the French Government were to insist on a time-limit of forty-eight hours to run from midday tomorrow, *it would be impossible for the Government to hold the situation here.* (*British Documents* 3, VII, 740.)

LORD HALIFAX telephoned Bonnet and said that:

. . . it was essential to make some announcement this evening *owing to the difficult position which had arisen in the House of Commons* . . . (*British Documents* 3, VII, 741.)

The British ultimatum was delivered on the morning of 3 September 1939. It expired at 11 a.m. without the Germans having replied to it. From that moment, until 8 May 1945, Britain was at war again with Germany.

Six minutes after midday on 3 September NEVILLE CHAMBERLAIN read to the House of Commons the British ultimatum, which had been delivered in Berlin by Sir Nevile Henderson:

'Sir, in the communication which I had the honour to make to you on 1st September, I informed you . . . that unless the German Government were prepared to give His Majesty's Government . . . satisfactory assurances that the German Government had suspended all aggressive action against Poland and were prepared promptly to withdraw their forces from Polish territory, His Majesty's Government . . . would, without hesitation, fulfil their obligations to Poland.'

Although this communication was made more than 24 hours ago, no reply has been received, but German attacks upon Poland have been continued and intensified. I have, accordingly, the honour to inform you that unless not later than 11 a.m., British Summer Time, today, September 3rd, satisfactory assurances to the above effect have been given by the German Government and have reached His Majesty's Government in London, a state of war will exist between the two countries as from that hour.

NEVILLE CHAMBERLAIN then told the House:

This was the final Note. No such undertaking was received by the time stipulated, and, consequently, this country is at war with Germany. . . .

This is a sad day for all of us, and to none is it sadder than to me. Everything that I have worked for, everything that I have hoped for, everything that I have believed in during my public life, has crashed into ruins. There is only one thing left for me to do; that is, to devote what strength and powers I have to forwarding the victory of the cause for which we have to sacrifice so much. I cannot tell what part I may be allowed to play myself; I trust I may live to see the day when Hitlerism has been destroyed and a liberated Europe has been re-established. (*Hansard.*)

There was some surprise that Chamberlain had spoken so movingly about himself, but had said nothing about the Poles.

ARTHUR GREENWOOD followed, and spoke for more than the Labour Party when he said:

For 54 hours Poland has stood alone, at the portals of civilisation, defending us and all free nations, and all that we stand for, and all that we hold dear. She has stood with unexampled bravery, with epic heroism, before her hesitant friends have come to her aid. (*Hansard.*)

WINSTON CHURCHILL then spoke of the moral value of Britain having sought peace, and of having made repeated efforts to avoid war:

This moral conviction alone affords that ever-fresh resilience which renews the strength and energy of people in long, doubtful and dark days. Outside, the storms of war may blow and the lands may be lashed with the fury of its gales, but in our own hearts this Sunday morning there is peace. Our hands may be active, but our consciences are at rest. . . .

This is not a question of fighting for Danzig or fighting for Poland. We are fighting to save the whole world from the pestilence of Nazi tyranny and in defence of all that is most sacred to man. This is no war for domination or imperial aggrandisement or material gain; no war to shut any country out of its sunlight and means of progress. It is a war . . . to establish, on impregnable rocks, the rights of the individual, and it is a war to establish and revive the stature of man. (*Hansard.*)

MINISTERS AND AMBASSADORS

Prime Minister		*Foreign Secretary*	
		1905–16	Edward Grey
1908–16	Henry Herbert Asquith		
1916–22	David Lloyd George	1916–19	Arthur Balfour
		1919–24	Lord Curzon
1922–23	Andrew Bonar Law		
1923–24	Stanley Baldwin		
1924	J. Ramsay MacDonald	1924	J. Ramsay MacDonald
1924–29	Stanley Baldwin	1924–29	Austen Chamberlain
1929–35	J. Ramsay MacDonald	1929–31	Arthur Henderson
		1931	Lord Reading
		1931–35	John Simon
1935–37	Stanley Baldwin	1935	Samuel Hoare
		1935–38	Anthony Eden
1937–40	Neville Chamberlain		
		1938–40	Lord Halifax
1940–45	Winston Churchill	1940–45	Anthony Eden

Major British Ambassadors to Berlin

1920–26	Lord D'Abernon
1928–33	Sir Horace Rumbold
1933–37	Sir Eric Phipps
1937–39	Sir Nevile Henderson

Biographical Sketches

The following sketches contain short notes on all those whose speeches or writings are quoted in this volume. The letter B at the end of a biographical sketch indicates authorship of at least one book in the bibliography, including memoirs.

CLIFFORD ALLEN (1889–1939). Imprisoned during Great War as Conscientious Objector. Active in Labour politics 1912–29. Supported Ramsay MacDonald's attempt to form a National Government 1931. Created Baron 1932. Frequent lecturer and constant writer on foreign affairs 1933–39. B

LEOPOLD AMERY CH (1893–1955). On editorial staff of *The Times* 1899–1909. Assistant Secretary, War Cabinet, 1917. Staff of War Council, Versailles. Conservative MP 1911–45. Secretary of State for the Colonies 1924–29, and for India and Burma 1940–45. B

NORMAN ANGELL (born 1872). Editor, *Foreign Affairs*, 1928–31. Labour MP 1929–31. Knighted 1931. Nobel Peace Prize 1933. B

FRANK ASHTON-GWATKIN CB (born 1889). Diplomat and novelist. Head of the economic section of the Foreign Office. Accompanied Runciman to Prague and Chamberlain to Munich. B

WILLIAM ASTOR (born 1907). Conservative MP 1935–45 and 1951–52. Parliamentary Private Secretary to Sir Samuel Hoare 1936–39. Succeeded his father as Viscount 1952.

CLEMENT ATTLEE KG OM CH (born 1883). Served European War Gallipoli and France. First Labour Mayor of Stepney 1919. Labour MP 1922–55. Postmaster General 1931. Leader of the Opposition 1935–40. Deputy Prime Minister 1942–45. Prime Minister 1945–51. Created Earl 1955. B

STANLEY BALDWIN KG (1867–1947). Conservative MP 1908–37; Prime Minister 1923–24, 1924–29 and 1935–37. Created Earl 1937.

FRANK BARRY DSO (born 1890). Served Great War. Archdeacon of Egypt 1923. Canon of Westminster 1933–41. Chaplain to the King 1930–41. Bishop of Southwell since 1941.

VIOLET BONHAM CARTER DBE (born 1887). Daughter of H. H. Asquith, Prime Minister, 1908–16. Governor of BBC 1941–46. President of the Liberal Party Organisation 1945–47. Created Dame 1953.

ROBERT BOOTHBY KBE (born 1900). Conservative MP 1924–58; Parliamentary Private Secretary to Winston Churchill, then Chancellor of the Exchequer, 1926–29. Created Baron 1958. B

HORATIO BOTTOMLEY (1860–1933). Journalist, financier and politican. Floated a number of gold-mining companies in 1890s. Founded *John Bull* 1906. Liberal MP 1906–12 (when he went bankrupt) and 1918–22. Expelled from House of Commons after being found Guilty of fraudulent conversion. Imprisoned 1922–27.

ROBERT BRAND CMG (1878–1963). Financial adviser to Chairman of Supreme Economic Council, Paris Peace Conference. Head of British Food Mission to America 1941–44. Created Baron 1946. Director, Lazard Brothers. B

R. A. BUTLER CH (born 1902). Conservative MP 1929– . Under-Secretary of State for Foreign Affairs 1938–41. Minister of Education 1941–45. Deputy Prime Minister 1963. Foreign Secretary 1963.

ALEXANDER CADOGAN OM GCMG (born 1884). Foreign Office. Knighted 1934. Permanent Under-Secretary, Foreign Office, 1938–46. Permanent UK Representative, United Nations, 1946–50.

E. H. CARR CBE (born 1892). Foreign Office 1916–36. At Paris Peace Conference. Assistant Editor of *The Times* 1941–46. Fellow, Trinity College, Cambridge, 1955. B

LORD ROBERT CECIL CH QC (1864–1958). Son of the 3rd Marquess of Salisbury. Conservative MP 1906–10 and 1911–23. Created Viscount Cecil of Chelwood 1923. Minister of Blockade 1916–18; Chancellor of the Duchy of Lancaster 1924–27. President, League of Nations Union, 1923–45. B

AUSTEN CHAMBERLAIN KG (1863–1937). Conservative MP 1892–1937. Chancellor of the Exchequer 1903–06 and 1919–21. Secretary of State for Foreign Affairs 1924–29. B

NEVILLE CHAMBERLAIN (1869–1940). Educ.: Rugby; Mason College, Birmingham. Manager, Sisal Plantation, Bahamas, 1890–97; Lord Mayor of Birmingham 1915–16; Director General of National Service 1916–17. Conservative MP 1918–40. Chancellor of the Exchequer 1923–24 and 1931–37. Prime Minister 1937–40. B

WINSTON CHURCHILL KG OM CH (born 1874). Soldier, historian and statesman. Educ: Harrow and Sandhurst. First Lord of the Admiralty 1911–15 and 1939–40; Prime Minister 1940–45 and 1951–55. Knighted 1953. B

ALFRED DUFF COOPER GCMG DSO (1890–1954). Served Great War. Politician and historian. First Lord of the Admiralty 1937–38. Resigned in protest against Munich Agreement. Ambassador to France 1944–47. Created Viscount Norwich 1952. B

EYRE CROWE GCB GCMG (1864–1925). Entered Foreign Office 1885. Both his mother and his wife were German. Knighted 1911. Permanent Under-Secretary of State for Foreign Affairs 1920–25.

LORD CURZON KG GCSI GCIE (1859–1925). Conservative MP 1886–98. Viceroy of India 1899–1905; Secretary of State for Foreign Affairs 1919–24. Created Marquess Curzon of Kedleston 1921.

EDGAR D'ABERNON GCB GCMG (1857–1941). Served in Army 1877–82. Governor, Imperial Ottoman Bank, 1889–97. Conservative MP 1899–1906. Created Baron 1914. Ambassador to Germany 1920–26. Created Viscount 1926. B

HUGH DALTON (1887–1962). Served in Army during Great War. Labour MP 1924–31 and 1935–59. Minister of Economic Warfare 1940–42. Chancellor of the Exchequer 1945–47. Created Baron 1960. B

GEOFFREY DAWSON (1874–1944). Colonial Office 1898–1901. Editor of *The Times* 1912–19 and 1923–41.

BARRY DOMVILE KBE CB CMG (born 1878). Entered Navy 1892. Rear-Admiral 1927. Director of Naval Intelligence 1927–30. Knighted 1934. B

ERIC DRUMMOND GCMG (1876–1951). Secretary General to the League of Nations 1919–32; Ambassador to Italy 1933–39. Succeeded half-brother as Earl of Perth. Deputy Leader of Liberal Party in House of Lords 1946–51.

ANTHONY EDEN KG MC (born 1897). Served Great War in France. Conservative MP 1923–57. Minister for League of Nations Affairs 1935. Secretary of State for Foreign Affairs 1935–38; for Dominion Affairs 1939–40; for War 1940 and for Foreign Affairs 1940–45 and 1951–55. Prime Minister 1955–57. Created Earl of Avon 1962.

LORD ESHER GCB GCVO (1852–1930). Liberal MP 1880–85; Governor of Windsor Castle 1928–30; Permanent Member Committee of Imperial Defence. B

H. A. L. FISHER OM (1865–1940). Politician and historian. Liberal MP 1916–26. President of the Board of Education 1916–22. A British Delegate to the League of Nations 1920–22. Warden of New College Oxford 1925–40. B

WILLIAM GALLACHER (born 1881). Communist MP 1935–50. President, Communist Party, since 1956.

J. L. GARVIN CH (died 1947). Editor-in-Chief, *Encyclopaedia Britannica* 1926–29; Editor of *The Observer* 1908–42. B

GEORGE V (1865–1936). Served in the Navy 1883–1892. Created Duke of York 1892. 1893 married Princess Mary of Teck. King 1910–36.

VICTOR GOLLANCZ (born 1893). Founded Victor Gollancz Ltd. publishing house 1928. Founded Left Book Club 1933, to combat Nazism. Chairman, National Campaign for the Abolition of Capital Punishment, 1955–56. B

ROBERT GRAVES (born 1895). Poet. Served Great War in France. Professor of Poetry, Oxford, 1916–63. B

ARTHUR GREENWOOD CH (1880–1954). Labour MP 1922–31 and 1932–54. Minister of Health 1929–31. Member of the War Cabinet 1940–42. Chairman of the Labour Party 1952. B

DAVID GRENFELL CBE (born 1881). Worked underground in coal mine 1893–1916. Labour MP 1922–59. Secretary for Mines 1940–42. 'Father of the House of Commons' 1953–59.

EDWARD GREY KG (1862–1933). Sent down from Oxford for 'incorrigible idleness' 1884. Liberal MP 1885–1916; Foreign Secretary 1905–16. Created Viscount 1916. President, League of Nations Union, 1918–33.

LORD HALIFAX KG OM GCSI GCMG GCIE (1881–1959). Conservative MP 1910–25. Created Baron Irwin 1925. Viceroy of India 1926–31. Succeeded father as Viscount Halifax 1934. Secretary of State for Foreign Affairs 1938–40. Ambassador to the United States 1941–46. Created Earl 1944. B

IAN HANNAH (1874–1944). British born. Taught in China, South Africa and Canada. Professor of Church History, Oberlin College, Ohio 1915–25. Conservative MP 1935–44. B

ARTHUR HENDERSON QC (born 1893). Served Great War. Labour MP 1923–24, 1929–31, 1935–51. Secretary of State for Air 1947–51.

NEVILE HENDERSON GCMG (1882–1942). Diplomatic Service 1905. Ambassador to Germany 1937–39. Group Commander, Home Guard, 1941–42. B

HERBERT HENSLEY HENSON (1863–1947). Bishop of Durham 1920–39. B

A. P. HERBERT (born 1890). Poet and humorist. Served Great War, Gallipoli and France (wounded). Joined Staff of *Punch* 1924. Independent MP 1935–50. Knighted 1945.

ADOLF HITLER (1889–1945). Served in Great War—wounded and gassed. Leader of the German Nazi Party. Chancellor 1933–45. Head of the German Armed Forces 1938–45. B

SAMUEL HOARE GCSI GBE (1880–1959). Conservative MP 1910–44. Secretary of State for Air 1922–24, 1924–29 and 1940. Secretary of State for Foreign Affairs 1935. Held Cabinet office 1923–24, 1924–29 and 1931–40. Ambassador to Spain 1940–44. Created Viscount Templewood 1944. B

LESLIE HORE-BELISHA (1893–1957). Served in Army during Great War. Liberal MP 1923–42. Secretary of State for War 1938–40. A critic of Churchill's conduct of the war. Independent MP 1942–45. Created Baron 1954.

GRAHAM SETON HUTCHINSON DSO MC (1890–1946). Soldier and historian. Served Great War (wounded three times). First Principal, Shri Shivaji Military School, Poona. Worked in Air Ministry 1939. B

THOMAS INSKIP KC (1876–1947). Naval Intelligence 1915–18. Conservative MP 1918–39. Knighted 1922. Solicitor-General 1922. Minister for the Co-ordination of Defence 1936–39. Created Viscount 1940. Lord Chief Justice 1940–46.

WILLIAM EDMUND IRONSIDE GBE CMG DSO (1880–1959). Entered Royal Artillery 1899. C-in-C British Forces in Russia 1918–19; Knighted 1919. General 1935. G.O.C-in-C Eastern Command 1936–38. A.D.C.-General to King George VI 1937–40; Inspector-General, Overseas

Forces, 1939. Chief of the Imperial General Staff 1939–40; Field-Marshal 1940. Created Baron 1941.

ARCHIBALD JAMES KBE MC (born 1893). Served Army and R.A.F. 1914–26 (Wing-Commander.) Conservative MP 1931–45. Parliamentary Private Secretary to R. A. Butler 1936–38. Knighted 1945.

THOMAS JONES CH (1870–1955). Deputy Secretary to the Cabinet. Hon. Trustee, *The Observer*. B

HOWARD KENNARD GCMG (1878–1955). Entered Diplomatic Service 1901. Knighted 1929. Ambassador to Poland 1935–41.

JOSEPH KENWORTHY (1886–1953). Served in Navy 1902–20 (Lieut. Commander). Liberal MP 1919–26; Labour MP 1926–31. Succeeded father as Baron Strabolgi 1934. Opposition Chief Whip, House of Lords, 1938–42. B

J. M. KEYNES CB (1883–1946). Economist. Principal Treasury Representative at the Paris Peace Conference 1919; leading negotiator of the American loan to Britain 1945. Created Baron 1942. B

JOSEPH KING (1860–1943). Labour MP 1910–18. B

RUDYARD KIPLING (1865–1936). Novelist and poet. Lived in India 1882–89. Awarded Nobel Prize for Literature 1907. A cousin of Stanley Baldwin. His only son was killed in action 1915. B

GEORGE LANSBURY (1859–40). Educ: Elementary Day Schools. Labour MP 1910–12 and 1922–40. Leader of Labour Party 1931–35. B

WYNDHAM LEWIS (1884–1957). Educ: Slade School. Author and artist. Adviser to the Library of Congress, USA. B

DAVID LLOYD GEORGE OM (1863–1945). Educ: a Welsh Church School. Liberal MP 1890–1945. Prime Minister 1916–22. Created Earl 1945. B

LORD LONDONDERRY (1878–1949). Conservative MP 1906–15. Succeeded father as Marquess of Londonderry 1915. Secretary of State for Air 1931–35. B

EDITH LADY LONDONDERRY DBE (1879–1959). Wife of the 7th Marquess of Londonderry whom she married in 1899. Founder and Director-General, Women's Legion, 1914. First woman to be given the military DBE. B

COLONEL WILLIAM LONG (1868–1943). Served South African War. Brother of Walter Long, Conservative politician and First Lord of the Admiralty 1919–21.

PERCY LORAINE GCMG (1880–1961). Served South African War. Entered Diplomatic Service 1904. At Paris Peace Conference. Knighted 1925. Ambassador to Italy 1939–40.

LORD LOTHIAN KT CH (1882–1940). Secretary to Lloyd George, 1917–21. Held office in the National Government 1931–32. Ambassador to the United States 1939–40. B

J. RAMSAY MACDONALD (1866–1937). Educ: at a Board School. Secretary of Labour Party 1900–12; Labour MP 1906–18 and 1922–37. Prime Minister and Secretary of State for Foreign Affairs 1924 (Labour Government). Prime Minister 1929–35 (National Government).

HAROLD MACMILLAN (born 1894). Served Great War (wounded three times). Conservative MP 1924–29 and 1931–   . Chancellor of the Exchequer 1955–57. Prime Minister 1957–63. B

LOUIS MACNEICE CBE (1907–63). Poet and writer. Lecturer in Classics, Birmingham University 1930–36. B

GEOFFREY LE M. MANDER (1882–1962). Liberal MP 1929–45. Parliamentary Private Secretary to the Secretary of State for Air (Sir Archibald Sinclair) 1942–45. Knighted 1945.

THOMAS MOORE CBE (—). Regular Army 1908–25. Served Great War France and Ireland. Served in Russia 1918–20. Conservative MP since 1925. Knighted 1937. Created Baronet 1956.

EDGAR MOWRER (born 1892). Berlin and Paris correspondent of the *Chicago Daily News* during inter-war years. Deputy-Director, U.S. Office of War Information 1942–43. B

RAMSAY MUIR (1872–1941). Historian and politician. Liberal MP 1923–24. President of the National Liberal Federation 1933–36. B

GEOFFREY MURE MC (born 1893). Served Great War, France and Belgium. Fellow of Merton College 1922. Warden of Merton 1947–63.

GILBERT MURRAY OM (1866–1957). Professor of Greek, Oxford, 1908–36; Chairman, League of Nations Union, 1923–38. B

BENITO MUSSOLINI (1883–1945). Editor Socialist newspaper *Avanti*. Founder of the Italian Fascist Party. President of the Council of Ministers 1922–26. Prime Minister 1926–43. B

HAROLD NICOLSON KCVO CMG (born 1886). Diplomat, politician and author. Foreign Office 1909–29. Served on British delegation to Paris Peace Conference. MP (National Labour) 1935–45. Knighted 1953. B

CLIFFORD NORTON KCMG CVO (born 1891). Served Great War— Gallipoli and Palestine. Entered Diplomatic Service 1921. Private Secretary to Sir Robert Vansittart 1930–37. Counsellor, Warsaw, 1937–39. Knighted 1946. Ambassador to Greece 1946–51.

WILLIAM ORMSBY-GORE KG GCMG (born 1885). Conservative MP 1910–38. At Paris Peace Conference (Delegate in Middle East Section). Secretary of State for the Colonies 1936–38. Succeeded father as Baron Harlech, 1938.

ERIC PHIPPS GCB GCMG GCVO (1875–1945). Entered Foreign Office 1899. Minister, Paris 1922–28 and Vienna 1928–33. Knighted 1927. Ambassador to Germany 1933–37.

G. WARD PRICE (—). *Daily Mail* War Correspondent, Balkan War, 1912. Director, Associated Newspapers Ltd. (*Daily Mail, Daily Sketch, Evening News*). War Correspondent, France, 1939. B

VICTOR RAIKES KBE (born 1901). Conservative MP 1931–57. Knighted 1953.

ELEANOR RATHBONE (1873–1946). President, National Union for Equal Citizenship, 1919–29. Independent MP 1929–46. Vice-Chairman National Committee for Rescue from Nazi Terror. B

STEPHEN ROBERTS CMG (born 1901). Professor of Modern History, Sydney, 1929–47. Principal, Sydney University since 1947. B

HORACE RUMBOLD BT GCB GCMG MVO (1869–1941). Entered Diplomatic Service 1888. Chargé d'Affaires, Berlin, July 1914; Knighted 1917. British Minister, Berne, 1916–19. Ambassador to Germany 1928–33.

WALTER RUNCIMAN (1870–1949). Liberal MP 1899–1900, 1902–18, 1924–37. President of the Board of Trade 1914–16 and 1931–37. Created Viscount 1937.

BERTRAND RUSSELL OM (born 1872). Philosopher. Fellow, Trinity College, Cambridge. Imprisoned as conscientious objector 1918. Succeeded brother as Earl 1931. Nobel Prize for Literature 1950. B

ORME SARGENT GCMG KCB (1884–1962). Entered Foreign Office 1906. Knighted 1937. Permanent Under-Secretary, Foreign Office, 1946–49.

JOHN SIMON GCSI GCVO (1873–1954). Liberal MP 1906–18 and 1922–40. Secretary of State for Foreign Affairs 1931–35. Chancellor of the Exchequer 1937–40. Created Viscount 1940. B

ARCHIBALD SINCLAIR KT CMG (born 1890). Entered Army 1910. Served Great War (France). Succeeded grandfather as Baronet 1912. Liberal MP 1922–45. Leader, Liberal Parliamentary Party, 1935–45. Secretary of State for Air 1940–45. Created Viscount Thurso 1952.

H. WICKHAM STEED (1871–1956). Foreign Editor, *The Times*, 1914–19; Editor 1919–22. B

WILLIAM STRANG GCB GCMG (born 1893). Entered Foreign Office 1919. Permanent Under-Sectretary of State, Foreign Office, 1949–53. Created Baron 1954. Chairman, Royal Institute of International Affairs, 1958. B

LORD SWINTON GBE CH MC (born 1884). Served in Army 1914–17. Conservative MP 1918–35. Created Viscount Swinton 1935. Secretary of State for Air 1935–38. Held Cabinet office 1942–45 and 1951–55. Created Earl 1955. B

R. H. TAWNEY (1880–1962). Professor of Economic History, London University 1931–49. Adviser, British Embassy Washington, 1941–42.

A. J. P. TAYLOR (born 1906). Fellow and Tutor in Modern History, Magdalen College, Oxford, 1938–63. B

A. C. TEMPERLEY CB CMG DSO (1877–1940). Entered Army 1900. Military Representative at the League of Nations 1925–35. Military Correspondent of the *Daily Telegraph* 1935–39. B

JIM THOMAS (1903–60). Conservative MP 1931–55. Parliamentary Private Secretary to Anthony Eden 1937–38. First Lord of the Admiralty 1951–56. Created Viscount Cilcennin 1955.

ARNOLD TOYNBEE CH (born 1889). At Paris Peace Conference. Director of Studies, Royal Institute of International Affairs, 1925–55. B

ROBERT VANSITTART GB GCMG (1881–1957). Entered Foreign Office 1902. Secretary to Lord Curzon (then Foreign Secretary) 1920–24. Principal Private Secretary to the Prime Minister 1928–30. Knighted 1929. Permanent Under-Secretary, Foreign Office, 1930–38. Chief Diplomatic Adviser to the Foreign Secretary 1938–41. Created Baron 1941. B

A. LAMBERT WARD CVO DSO (1875–1956). Served Great War (Colonel; three times wounded). Conservative MP 1918–45. Comptroller H. M. Household 1936–37. Created Baronet 1929.

JOHN WARDLAW-MILNE KBE (—). Member Bombay Municipal Corporation 1907–17. Director, Bank of Bombay. Served Great War, (Lt. Col.). Conservative MP 1922–45. Knighted 1932. Member, Imperial Economic Committee, 1926–29. Chairman, Conservative Foreign Affairs Committee, 1939–45.

JOSIAH WEDGWOOD DSO (1872–1943). Served South African and Great Wars. Wounded at Dardanelles. Labour MP 1906–42. Chancellor of Duchy of Lancaster 1924. Created Baron 1942. B

JOHN WHEELER BENNETT KCVO CMG OBE (born 1902) Historian. Founder and Editor, *Bulletin of International News* 1924–32. Knighted 1959. B

CLIVE WIGRAM GCB GCVO (1873–1960). Served in Army 1893–1919. ADC to Lord Curzon (when Viceroy of India) 1899–1904. Private Secretary to King George V 1931–35. Knighted 1928. Created Baron 1935. Lord in Waiting to King George VI 1936–52 and to Queen Elizabeth II 1952–60.

JOHN WILMOT (born 1895). Served Royal Naval Air Service in Great War. Labour MP 1933–35 and 1939–50. Minister of Supply 1945–47. Created Baron 1950.

ARNOLD WILSON KCIE CSI CMG DSO (1884–1940). Entered Army 1903. Indian Political Department 1909. Political Resident in Persian Gulf 1918–20. Conservative MP 1933–40. Enlisted as tail-gunner, RAF, and killed in action 1940. B

HORACE WILSON GCB GCMG CBE (born 1882). Entered Civil Service 1900. Knighted 1924. Chief Industrial Adviser to H.M. Govt. 1930–39 Head of H.M. Civil Service 1939–42.

EARL WINTERTON (1883–1962). Served Great War, Gallipoli and Palestine. Conservative MP 1904–51. Chancellor of the Duchy of Lancaster 1937–39, with a seat in the Cabinet 1938–39. B

EVELYN WRENCH KCMG (born 1882). Engaged in journalism 1904–12. Chief Private Secretary to Air Minister 1917–18. Founder, English-speaking Union, 1918. Editor, *The Spectator*, 1925–32. Knighted 1932. B

ALFRED ZIMMERN (1879–1957). Political Intelligence Dept. Foreign Office 1918–19. Professor of International Relations, Oxford, 1930–44. Knighted 1936. Deputy Director, Foreign Office Research Department, 1943–45. B

Bibliography

This bibliography is divided into five sections. The first section contains nine works of reference, all of which can be obtained from Public Libraries. Oakeshott's *The Social and Political Doctrines of Contemporary Europe* is available in most school and university libraries. The second section contains books written between 1914 and 1942. Their authors are all mentioned in the biographical sketches at the beginning of this book, and in the text of the book itself. The third and fourth sections contain the autobiographies and biographies of many of the politicians mentioned in the text. The fifth section consists of books written after 1942, mostly by historians, dealing with the problems that have arisen in the book. This section also contains a number of reflective works by those who were concerned with inter-war events.

A. REFERENCE BOOKS

Parliamentary Debates (Hansard). H.M.S.O.

Survey of International Affairs by Arnold Toynbee and others. Covers 1920–39. Oxford.

Documents on International Affairs, ed. J. W. Wheeler-Bennett and others. Covers 1923–39. Oxford U.P.

Dictionary of National Biography, 4 vols. 1901–1950. Oxford U.P.

Documents on British Foreign Policy. H.M.S.O. (referred to as *British Documents*).

Documents on German Foreign Policy 1918–45. H.M.S.O.

Who's Who. Published annually. A. & C. Black.

Who Was Who. From 1897. A. & C. Black.

M. Oakeshott. *The Social and Political Doctrines of Contemporary Europe*. Cambridge, U.P. 1939.

B. CONTEMPORARY WORKS

1914

GILBERT MURRAY. *How Can War Ever Be Right?* Oxford U.P.

H. A. L. FISHER. *The War: Its Causes and Issues*. Longmans

RAMSAY MUIR. *Britain's Case Against Germany*. Manchester Univ. Press

RAMSAY MUIR. *The National Principle and the War*. Oxford U.P.

D. LLOYD GEORGE. *Honour and Dishonour*. Methuen

1915

HERBERT HENSON. *War-time Sermons*. Macmillan

ARNOLD TOYNBEE. *Nationality and the War*. Dent

1917

ARNOLD TOYNBEE. *The German Terror in Belgium*. Hodder & Stoughton

1918

GILBERT MURRAY. *Faith War and Policy*. Oxford U.P.

1919

J. L. GARVIN. *The Economic Foundations of Peace*. Macmillan

1920

J. M. KEYNES. *The Economic Consequences of the Peace*. Labour Research Department

JOSEPH KING. *Political Crooks at the Peace Conference*. Indep. Labour Party

1921

R. H. BRAND. *War and National Finance*. Arnold

G. S. HUTCHINSON. *The Thirty Third Division in France and Flanders*. Waterlow

NORMAN ANGELL. *The Fruits of Victory*. Collins

GILBERT MURRAY. *The Problem of Foreign Policy*. Allen & Unwin

1922

J. M. KEYNES. *A Revision of the Treaty*. Macmillan

ALFRED ZIMMERN. *Europe in Convalescence*. Mills & Boon

1923

NEVILLE CHAMBERLAIN. *Norman Chamberlain: A Memoir*. John Murray

WINSTON CHURCHILL. *The World Crisis*, vol. 1. Butterworth

RUDYARD KIPLING. *The Irish Guards in the Great War*. 2 vols. Macmillan

1924

JOSEPH KING. *The Ruhr: History of the French Occupation.* British Bureau for Ruhr Information

1925

J. WHEELER-BENNETT. *Information on the Reduction of Armaments.* Allen and Unwin

1927

JOSEPH KENWORTHY. *Will Civilisation Crash?* Benn

1928

HUGH DALTON. *Towards the Peace of Nations.* Routledge
AUSTEN CHAMBERLAIN. *Peace in Our Times.* Allan
LORD ROBERT CECIL. *The Way of Peace.* Allan
BENITO MUSSOLINI. *My Autobiography.* Hutchinson

1929

ROBERT GRAVES. *Goodbye to All That.* Cassell

1930

LORD D'ABERNON. *Foreign Policy.* Oxford U.P.
J. WHEELER BENNETT. *Information on the Reparation Settlement.* Allen & Unwin
RAMSAY MUIR. *Political Consequences of the Great War.* Butterworth
JOSEPH KENWORTHY. *New Wars, New Weapons.* Mathews & Marrot

1931

WYNDHAM LEWIS. *Hitler.* Chatto & Windus

1932

WINSTON CHURCHILL. *Thoughts and Adventures.* Butterworth
D. LLOYD GEORGE. *The Truth about Reparations and War Debts.* Heinemann
J. WHEELER BENNETT. *Disarmament and Security Since Locarno*

1933

EDGAR MOWRER. *Germany Puts the Clock Back.* Bodley Head
ADOLF HITLER. *Mein Kampf.* Hurst & Blackett

NORMAN ANGELL. *The Great Illusion 1933.* Heinemann
D. LLOYD GEORGE. *War Memoirs*, vol. 1. Odhams
J. WHEELER-BENNETT. *The Wreck of Reparations.* Allen & Unwin
JOSEPH KING. *The German Revolution.* Williams & Norgate
HAROLD NICOLSON. *Peacemaking 1919.* Constable

1934

GILBERT MURRAY. *The Cult of Violence.* Lovat Dickson
WICKHAM STEED. *Hitler: Whence and Whither.* Nisbet
J. WHEELER-BENNETT. *The Disarmament Deadlock.* Routledge
ALFRED ZIMMERN. *British Foreign Policy Since the War.* Univ. Coll.
Nottingham

1935

AUSTEN CHAMBERLAIN. *Down The Years.* Cassell
LORD LOTHIAN. *Pacifism is not Enough (Nor Patriotism Either).* Oxford
U.P.

1936

HERBERT HENSON. *Christian Morality.*
BERTRAND RUSSELL. *Which Way to Peace.* Michael Joseph
BARRY DOMVILE. *By and Large.* Hutchinson
WICKHAM STEED. *Vital Peace.* Constable
ARNOLD WILSON. *Walks and Talks Abroad.* Oxford U.P.
ALFRED ZIMMERN. *The League of Nations and the Rule of Law*
HERBERT HENSON. *Abyssinia: Reflections of an Onlooker.* Hugh Rees

1937

WINSTON CHURCHILL. *Great Contemporaries.* Butterworth
WYNDHAM LEWIS. *Count Your Dead: They are Alive.* Lovat Dickson
G. WARD PRICE. *I Know These Dictators.* Harrap
STEPHEN ROBERTS. *The House that Hitler Built.* Methuen
CLEMENT ATTLEE. *The Labour Party in Perspective.* Gollancz

1938

LORD LONDONDERRY. *Ourselves and Germany.* Robert Hale
CHARLES PETRIE. *The Chamberlain Tradition.* Right Book Club
NORMAN ANGELL. *Peace With the Dictators.* Hamish Hamilton
IAN HANNAH. *History of British Foreign Policy.* Nicholson & Watson
D. LLOYD GEORGE. *The Truth about the Peace Treaties.* Gollancz
GEORGE LANSBURY. *My Quest for Peace.* Michael Joseph

LOUIS MACNIECE. *Autumn Journal*. Faber & Faber
HAROLD NICOLSON. *National Character and National Policy*. Univ.
    Coll. Nottingham
ELEANOR RATHBONE. *War Can Be Averted*. Gollancz
A. C. TEMPERLEY. *The Whispering Gallery of Europe*. Collins
LORD ESHER. *Journals and Letters*, 4 vols. Nicholson and Watson

1939

L. S. AMERY. *The German Colonial Claim*. Longmans
NORMAN ANGELL. *For What Do We Fight?* Hamish Hamilton
A. DUFF COOPER. *The Second World War*. Jonathan Cape
WINSTON CHURCHILL. *Step By Step*. Butterworth
VICTOR GOLLANCZ. *Is Mr Chamberlain Saving Peace?* Gollancz
WYNDHAM LEWIS. *The Jews—Are They Human?* Allen & Unwin
HAROLD MACMILLAN. *Economic Aspects of Defence*. Macmillan
HAROLD NICOLSON. *Marginal Comment*. Constable
G. WARD PRICE. *Year of Reckoning*. Cassell
WYNDHAM LEWIS. *The Hitler Cult*. Dent
WICKHAM STEED. *Our War Aims*. Secker & Warburg
ALFRED ZIMMERN. *Spiritual Values and World Affairs*. Oxford U.P.
RAMSAY MUIR. *Future For Democracy*. Nicholson & Watson
E. H. CARR. *The Twenty Years Crisis*. Macmillan

1940

WINSTON CHURCHILL. *Into Battle*. Cassell
NORMAN ANGELL. *Why Freedom Matters*. Penguin Books
GEORGE LANSBURY. *This Way to Peace*. Rich & Cowan
HUGH DALTON. *Hitler's War: Before and After*. Penguin Books
HAROLD NICOLSON. *Why Britain Is At War*. Penguin Books
H. A. L. FISHER, HAROLD NICOLSON and others. *The Background and
    Issues of the War*. Oxford U.P.
EVELYN WRENCH. *I Loved Germany*. Michael Joseph
NEVILE HENDERSON. *Failure of a Mission*. Hodder & Stoughton
ARTHUR GREENWOOD. *Why We Fight: Labour's Case*. Routledge
RAMSAY MUIR. *Civilisation and Liberty*. Jonathan Cape

1941

LORD VANSITTART. *Black Record: Germans Past and Present*. Hamish
    Hamilton

1942

E. H. CARR. *Conditions of Peace*. Macmillan

WICKHAM STEED. *That Bad Man—Hitler*

WINSTON CHURCHILL. *The Unrelenting Struggle*. Cassell

C. AUTOBIOGRAPHIES AND PERSONAL PAPERS

L. S. AMERY. *My Political Life*. Hutchinson. 1955. 3 vols.

NORMAN ANGELL. *After All*. Hamish Hamilton. 1951

CLEMENT ATTLEE. *As It Happened*. Heinemann. 1954

ROBERT BOOTHBY. *I Fight to Live*. Gollancz. 1947

LORD ROBERT CECIL. *A Great Experiment*. Jonathan Cape. 1941

LORD ROBERT CECIL. *All The Way*. Hodder & Stoughton. 1949

A. DUFF COOPER (Viscount Norwich). *Old Men Forget*. Hart-Davis. 1953

LORD D'ABERNON. *An Ambassador of Peace*. Hodder & Stoughton. 1929–30

HUGH DALTON. *The Fateful Years*. Muller. 1957

ANTHONY EDEN (Lord Avon). *Facing The Dictators*. Cassell. 1962

LORD HALIFAX. *Fulness of Days*. Collins. 1957

LORD HALIFAX. *Speeches on Foreign Policy*, ed. H. H. E. Craster. Oxford U.P. 1940

NEVILE HENDERSON. *Water Under the Bridges*. Hodder & Stoughton. 1945

SAMUEL HOARE (Viscount Templewood). *Nine Troubled Years*. Collins. 1954

W. E. IRONSIDE. *The Ironside Diaries*, ed. R. Macleod. Constable. 1962

LESLIE HORE-BELISHA. *Private Papers*, ed. R. J. Minney, Collins. 1960

THOMAS JONES. *Diary With Letters*. Oxford U.P. 1954

IVONE KIRKPATRICK. *The Inner Circle*. Macmillan. 1959

LADY LONDONDERRY. *Retrospect*. Muller. 1938

LORD LONDONDERRY. *Wings of Destiny*. Macmillan. 1943

LORD SIMON. *Retrospect*. Hutchinson. 1952

LORD SNOWDEN. *An Autobiography*. Nicholson & Watson. 1934

LORD STRANG. *Home and Abroad*. Deutsch. 1956

LORD SWINTON. *I Remember*. Hutchinson. 1948

LORD VANSITTART. *The Mist Procession*. Hutchinson. 1958

JOSIAH WEDGWOOD. *Memoirs of a Fighting Life*. Hutchinson. 1941

LORD WINTERTON. *Fifty Tumultuous Years*. Hutchinson. 1955

D. BIOGRAPHIES

A. W. BALDWIN. *My Father: The True Story*. Allen & Unwin. 1956

J. R. M. BUTLER. *Lord Lothian*. Macmillan. 1960

KEITH FEILING. *Neville Chamberlain*. Macmillan. 1946

ROY HARROD. *John Maynard Keynes*. Macmillan. 1951

A. CAMPBELL JOHNSON. *Viscount Halifax*. Robert Hale. 1941

THOMAS JONES. *Lloyd George*. Oxford U.P. 1951

IAIN MACLEOD. *Neville Chamberlain*. Muller. 1961

ARTHUR MARWICK. *Clifford Allen: The Open Conspirator*. Oliver & Boyd. 1964

HAROLD NICOLSON. *Curzon: The Last Phase*. Constable. 1934

HAROLD NICOLSON. *George V*. Constable. 1962

FRANK OWEN. *Tempestuous Journey* (Lloyd George). Hutchinson. 1954

CHARLES PETRIE. *The Life and Letters of the Rt. Hon. Sir Austen Chamberlain*. Cassell. 1940

RAYMOND POSTGATE. *The Life of George Lansbury*. Longmans. 1951

MARY STOCKS. *Eleanor Rathbone*. Gollancz. 1950

J. WHEELER-BENNETT. *George VI*. Macmillan. 1958

EVELYN WRENCH. *Geoffrey Dawson and Our Times*. Hutchinson. 1955

G. M. YOUNG. *Stanley Baldwin*. Hart-Davis. 1952

IAN COLVIN. *Lord Vansittart*. Gollancz. 1964

E. HISTORICAL PERSPECTIVES

F. T. A. ASHTON-GWATKIN. *The British Foreign Office*. Syracuse Univ. Press. 1949

ALAN BULLOCK. *Hitler: A Study in Tyranny*. Odhams. 1952

R. BASSETT. *Democracy and Foreign Policy*. Longmans. 1952

E. H. CARR. *The Twenty Years Crisis 1919–1939*. Macmillan. 1942

WINSTON CHURCHILL. *The Gathering Storm*. Cassell. 1948

W. and Z. COATES. *A History of Anglo-Soviet Relations*. Lawrence & Wishart. 1943

G. M. GATHORNE-HARDY. *A Short History of International Affairs 1920–39*, 4th edition. Oxford U.P. 1950

MARTIN GILBERT and RICHARD GOTT. *The Appeasers*. Weidenfeld & Nicolson. 1963

R. B. MCCALLUM. *Public Opinion and the Last Peace*. Oxford. 1944

ARTHUR MURRAY (Lord Elibank). *Reflections on Some Aspects of British Foreign Policy Between the two World Wars*. Oliver & Boyd. 1946

L. B. NAMIER. *Diplomatic Prelude 1938–39*. Macmillan. 1948

P. A. REYNOLDS. *British Foreign Policy in the Inter-War Years*. Longmans. 1954

E. M. ROBERTSON. *Hitler's Pre-war Policy*. Longmans. 1963

WALFORD SELBY. *Diplomatic Twilight*. John Murray. 1953

LORD STRANG. *Britain in World Affairs*. Faber–Deutsch. 1961

A. J. P. TAYLOR. *The Course of German History*. Hamish Hamilton. 1945

A. J. P. TAYLOR. *The Origins of the Second World War*. Hamish Hamilton. 1961

HUGH THOMAS. *Spanish Civil War*. Eyre & Spottiswoode. 1961

R. H. ULLMAN. *Intervention and the War*. Oxford U.P. 1961

LORD VANSITTART. *Lessons of My Life*. Hutchinson. 1943

F. P. WALTERS. *The League of Nations*. Oxford U.P. 1952

V. WELLESLEY. *Diplomacy in Fetters*. Hutchinson. 1944

J. WHEELER-BENNETT. *Munich: Prologue to Tragedy*. Macmillan. 1948

Index

Note: The page numbers in bold type refer to the biographical sketches of the person concerned.